EMBRACING
Asperger's

of related interest

Asperger's Syndrome
A Guide for Parents and Professionals
2nd edition
Tony Attwood
ISBN 978 1 84310 307 3

The Complete Guide to Asperger's Syndrome
Tony Attwood
ISBN 978 1 84310 669 2

Kids in the Syndrome Mix of ADHD, LD, Asperger's,
Tourette's, Bipolar, and More!
The one stop guide for parents, teachers, and other professionals
Martin Kutscher
ISBN 978 1 84310 810 8 (hardback)
ISBN 978 1 84310 811 5 (paperback)

Freaks, Geeks and Asperger Syndrome
A User Guide to Adolescence
Luke Jackson
ISBN 978 1 84310 098 0

EMBRACING
Asperger's

A Primer for Parents and Professionals

Richard Bromfield, Ph.D.

Jessica Kingsley *Publishers*
London and Philadelphia

First published in 2011
by Jessica Kingsley Publishers
116 Pentonville Road
London N1 9JB, UK
and
400 Market Street, Suite 400
Philadelphia, PA 19106, USA

www.jkp.com

Library of Congress Cataloging in Publication Data
A CIP catalog record for this book is available from the Library of Congress

British Library Cataloguing in Publication Data
A CIP catalogue record for this book is available from the British Library

ISBN 978 1 84905 818 6

Printed and bound in the United States

Contents

Introduction

Who is this child? Who is this student?

If I tell you that he has a 125 IQ, do you know him? How about if I add that he has a unique neuropsychological profile with wide-ranging strengths and weaknesses? Do you sense that you know him when I say that he is socially awkward, preoccupied with airplanes, and prone to one-sided conversations? How about when you hear that he doesn't like sunlight in his eyes, loves the smell of old books, and enjoys pressing his thumbs hard into the tips of his other fingers? And will you recognize him when I inform you that he's a bit clumsy, speaks with an adult's vocabulary, is awfully disorganized, and suffers colossal anxiety?

Like most of us, hearing this description will give you some sense of the child. You will begin to form an impression of him. And when you actually meet him in person, you probably will not be surprised by much of what you see and hear. When he starts to talk and recites in detail the weight and wingspan and flying range of military aircraft, you may nod to yourself. Just as you will when he avoids your eyes or sits rigidly and uncomfortably as if your mere presence poses danger to him. His relative lack of social etiquette and stilted way of talking will confirm what you're already fairly sure of.

Yes, you are right. This is a boy with Asperger syndrome. But just because you can rightly identify the child and the Asperger's, *does that mean you really know him?*

Think, for a moment, what it means to know a child who doesn't have Asperger's. Do we base our knowing that child on measures of intelligence, on IQ and achievement test scores? Probably not. How about on his eye gaze or hand-to-eye coordination? His proper use of pronouns or his ability to express his feelings? Instead of focusing on such finite and piecemeal data, our impressions will probably involve a much deeper, greater, and richer gestalt, a virtual potpourri of experiences with that child. If someone asked that we describe that child in a word or two, we'd be hard put. And yet we tend to rely on the term *Asperger's* to define and introduce who that other child is.

I'm giving the punchline away. But that is okay for this is no joke. For all of its diagnostic and clinical relevance, in many ways the term *Asperger's* utterly fails to tell us who a particular child is. More worrisome, in no way can that term tell us who that child is, all that child can be, or, for that important matter, who he himself wishes to become.

All of this peril, of course, occurs equally should you discover that the child with Asperger's I've been describing is actually a girl.

As you will soon read, my 30 years of clinical experience has taught me many undeniable truths about children with Asperger's:

- Children with Asperger's differ from every other child with or without Asperger's.

- They are much richer and more complex than has been realized.

- They have inner worlds, thoughts, and feelings that defy what older research and conventional wisdom about autism has presumed and advised us.

- Their more stereotypical behaviors are not reliable indicators of who they are, of what they think, feel, experience, know and so forth.

- Their communications with people, including with themselves, mean more to them than is assumed.

- They often are more capable of, interested in, and understanding of relationships than has been believed.

- Their neurological differences deny them critical opportunities for growth.

- What autism and clinical experts have tended to make of those neurological differences has further deprived these children of experiences that they crave and (developmentally) need.

- Concepts most germane to being human—such as feelings, empathy, and creativity—hold relevance to these children too.

- These children frequently smash through the glass ceilings that authoritative professionals have predicted for them (especially in the past).

- Any of us who ignore these truths deal a severe and cruel blow to these children's esteem, vitality, selfhood, and happiness.

My dramatic words understate the reality. I sense, however, that I am saying nothing new to the parents and teachers who know such children. That Asperger syndrome is a variant of autism is no longer news. That it is a neurological problem caused by biology, and not bad parenting, has been long and well established. And most readers, I suspect, agree fully with me that the child is a whole child, and not just a tally of discrete skills and scores. But this reality is easier headlined than seen, lived, and heeded in the (parenting or teaching) moment, day after day after day.

It is true that, at least for now, we have no cure for Asperger's or any other form of autism. Until we do, all we can do is to help alleviate the disorder as best we can. Parents and teachers who care for a child with Asperger's grasp and lament the stress, hurt, and hardship that can fall upon the child and, by proxy, his family. And so they, parents and teachers, ever strive to help the child overcome brain-given difficulties in the processing of language, feelings, and social interaction. These loving and caring adults throw all of their being and might into methods that might help the child to make friends, carry on mutual conversation, say socially fitting things, reduce impulsive and aggressive behaviors, and so forth. Their common goal, at its heart, is to help the child live a life more and more like the life that children without Asperger's know. (I will later address the not-to-be-ignored question as to whether people with Asperger's even want to be what others consider to be "improved" in these ways.)

For all of their merits and efficacy, however, where do these interventions leave the child's feelings, attitudes, thoughts, dreams, and all the intangible stuff of life, the precious goods of being that we cherish in other children and ourselves as gospel essentials for a meaningful and fulfilling existence? Where do they leave the child with experiences of life and himself that are very much colored by the biological realities of Asperger's, and that yet still need to be heard and seen, validated, empathized with, understood, and accepted? Where do they leave the child who, just as does his neurotypical peer, has to confront and negotiate all of the ordinary challenges of childhood, adolescence, and growing up? And, hardly last, where do they leave the child who, no less than any other child or person, has to develop a self and an identity? These questions, above all, lie at the heart of this book, my therapeutic approach, and this call to reflection and rethinking a new kind of action.

Readers should know that I did not come to my views overnight. As a psychologist who's been working with such children and their families for 30 years now, it has been the children themselves who—hour by hour, therapy by therapy—have shown me what is, what matters, and what can be done. Throughout the book you will hear bits and pieces of these children and my trek. After all, any parent of such children, and any teacher or therapist who works with such children, endure personal journeys toward understanding. I am no exception to that rule. My relationship to these children and to the whole concept of Asperger syndrome has evolved continually, and, I hope, it ever will.

My goals for the book are all at once lofty and realistic. My experience has taught me that parents and educators want information and insight, even when it challenges them. They want honesty and frankness, not sugar-coated pabulum that goes down easy but offers empty calories and false reassurance. Above all, parents and teachers seek *anything* that might bring greater understanding of the child. Parents and teachers alike know too well the feeling that they are not quite reaching the child, that they are not quite hearing and getting it, that they are not communicating just right or at all. Words can barely describe the accompanying frustration and heartache parents and teachers can feel. On the other hand, there is nothing in the world more thrilling, more heart-stirring, and more significant than those instances when parent and child, or teacher and child, connect.

My book aims to help parents and teachers alike to see and meet the psychological needs of the child with Asperger's. This implies deeply appreciating what Asperger's is like *for and to* the child himself or herself, in all of its glory and confusion—big, small, and minute. We'll watch what it means for such a child to grow a self and evolve an identity within the context of Asperger neurology. Though I will frequently offer suggestions or strategies that parents and teachers might find helpful, my larger hope is to expand their vision and senses, hearts and minds, to the "data" that children with Asperger's—like children without, and, for that matter, all people—ever transmit in hopes of being received and understood. My message and method is inspired by great and noble purpose, just as is your daily devotion as parent and educator. In fact, I suspect that many parent and teacher readers will find my book mostly confirming, putting into words what they have always themselves known and wanted others to understand. Together I am certain we can come closer to that wonderful and rewarding place and vision, and to children with Asperger's who grow ever more connected to themselves, others, and the world.

Note to Readers

Writing a book for parents is a sensitive matter. The subject of Asperger's—with its subtleties, complexities, and challenges—lends yet greater peril to that task. I know that, despite my best efforts, I will sometimes say something that offends or that you already know. I'd have liked to begin many of my observations with *as you may know*, but that repetition would soon grow tiresome. Please keep in mind that, as sure as anything, I am aware of how well-informed and well-studied the parents and teachers of these children tend to be.

Writing a book that addresses parents *and* teachers only added to my challenge. I know that these two populations of caregiving differ substantially. I am not equating them. Being a parent of a child with developmental issues is not the same as being the teacher of that child. And yet there is much in what parents and teachers share that compelled me to write this book for both.

Parents and educators spend considerable time with the child, as home and school together constitute much of a child's world. Parents and teachers bring attitudes that, while distinct, share much in terms of caring and dedication. Parents and teachers employ skills that can be honed and understanding that can be furthered, all for the child's benefit. Both parents and teachers strive to do their best by the child, and both must sort through what can be a mass and a mess of information and professional guidance. And, by virtue of sharing a child who can be challenging if not a downright enigma, both parents and teachers often know the same confusion, frustration, discouragement, and so on. This to me adds up to an all-encompassing comparison and reason to reach out to both populations of caregivers simultaneously. I hope that both parent and teacher readers will forgive me when I step on their toes or fail to give sufficient credit where due.

I also apologize to allied professionals whose therapies play such a significant role in advancing the child's speech, language, motor, and social skills. Though I do not devote the book explicitly to these professionals, know for sure that they play a critical role in the child's life and education, and wholly share in everything that this book discusses about children with Asperger's.

I also wish to talk about my use of terminology. Some experts distinguish Asperger's from High-Functioning Autism (HFA); some do not. I follow the lead of a 2009 review study that suggests Asperger's and HFA are diagnostically related, both belong on the autistic spectrum of disorders, and both can be discussed and addressed together (Witwer and Lecavelier 2008). For the sake of simplicity and readability, I mostly rely on the term *Asperger's*. More trivially, and for generic discussions, I randomly alternate gender to avoid the tedium of *he* and *she*, *him* and *her*. Of course, when focusing on differences between boys and girls with Asperger's, my use of gender will be specific and germane.

Last, please note that, in organizing and writing this book, I strove to build a case for my view, that is, to incrementally show parent and teacher readers what children with Asperger's have revealed to me over years of therapy hours. As a result, there may be discussions where it feels that I am *saying it again*. Please bear with me and such moments; I simply do not wish to risk my and the children's messages being lost in any contexts or forms.

Caution

While my perspective, I believe, holds much relevance for the child with Asperger's, it is not a substitute for well-founded and invaluable interventions that address behavior, speech and language, social pragmatics, peer interactions, organization, education, and so forth. My approach presents an attitude, posture, and way of being with the child that coexists—think *hovers*—alongside and around whatever the person, method, or program at hand. My approach is meant to support and enhance all that you do with the child as a parent, educator, or allied professional.

1

THE CHILD'S BURDEN

Consider this playground scene:

It is a crisp and sunny fall morning in New England. At one end of the elementary school field older boys play touch football, while a much larger group of boys and girls play soccer on the other half. Screaming children chase each other around, over and through the slides and climbing sets. Girls play on the swings and jump rope, all the while chatting and laughing. Children contest a fierce game of Four Square on the asphalt court. Seemingly happy, social, engaged, and active girls and boys appear to cover every inch of the playground. But look a bit further and we'll discover two other children.

There, several yards off the corner of the field, under the cover of some hanging trees, almost into the woods, we can make out a boy. James is busy weaving broken branches and twigs into a fort that he's worked on for the past three weeks. Though over that time several other boys visited to see what he was up to, James's lecturing them about war tactics and his sternly warning them not to "mess up his work" sent them away. (They had no idea that James secretly wanted other children to join him in his "mission.")

And there, nearer the social hubbub at the swings, a girl quietly sits on the edge of a concrete block, leaning up against a bike rack. Oblivious, so it appears, to the peers who talk and play around her, Nellie reads a book that she carries with her everywhere. Nothing short of an earthquake could disturb her focus. She reads the fifth book in a series about girls. She's read every one of the more than dozen books in the series many times over. She's already read this volume seven times and, so she told me, she planned to read it again—and probably again after that.

In order to grasp what Asperger syndrome means in the real world for real children, children like James and Nellie, we need to begin by revisiting its neurological basis and implications, a subject that many parents and educators are already experts on.

Though we could look to the psychiatric criteria of diagnosis, I think one of the most insightful models of what Asperger's is comes from a 1987 description of autism:

> Autism represents a syndrome or collection of symptoms originating primarily from a basic neurological deficit [...] in information processing and emotional communication, secondly, from "psychological defenses against states experienced as a result of those deficits, and [thirdly from a] lack of crucial socializing experiences." (Bemporad, Ratey and O'Driscoll 1987, as quoted in Bromfield 1989, p.448)

This is pretty abstract and full of jargon. What, we must ask, in plain English does this say and, more importantly, what does it mean for children with Asperger's, children like James and Nellie?

Foremost, it means that the child comes into the world with a brain and neurology less adept at dealing with emotions, social experience, and certain kinds of communication. Whatever the degree of impairment, such deficits have to be significant. Feelings, social connection, and language—verbal and nonverbal—are the oxygen that fuels human existence and experience. The child who goes through life with compromises in these central areas is bound to have it tougher, much tougher. Understanding who they are in relationship to other people is how children develop their unique selves and identities. If this were all that James and Nellie had to deal with, life would be challenging. But children with Asperger's have more to deal with—a lot more.

Primary and inborn deficits in processing language, feelings, and social experiences convey a secondary hardship as profound as the primary ones. Having in a daily way coped with impairments and their fallout, is it any wonder that James and Nellie naturally retreated into smaller and more restricted worlds where they could understand, control, and reckon life? As Tony Attwood wrote, trying to fit in socially can lead to "mental and physical exhaustion" (2007, p.17) and provoke children's running back to a place, like their homes and rooms, where the unrelenting demand eases. Being human, children with Asperger's cannot help but adapt and find ways to survive what are pervasive assaults on their self-esteems. Is it any wonder that children with Asperger's often pull away, to the escape of a computer, good book, or fort in the woods, where they can feel protected and safe, where they can socially and psychologically let their hair down?

And who can blame them? Attempting to approach and engage others, especially other children, can be one dismal failure after failure that can confuse, frustrate, humiliate, frighten, sadden, and hurt. How many times could you or I, supposedly healthy grownups, try and fail to do something before we wanted to give up and look elsewhere for our stimulation, interests, and companionship? How long could we willingly subject ourselves to an ordeal that seems a lot like hammering one's own thumb, only in this case it was James's and Nellie's total being that got hammered over and over.

But for all of this burden, James and Nellie carried much more on their child-sized backs. Being less agile at sharing language, feelings, and engagement, their child's world of experience grew ever smaller and smaller. Whereas other children's worlds expand, James's and Nellie's worlds shrunk. The child with deficits in communication tends to have fewer people to talk with. The child who lacks empathy and social skills tends to have fewer people to interact with. The child with Asperger's needs more practice to learn, grow, and rehearse social and communication skills. And yet, in a cruel irony that typifies so much of life, the child typically has rarer and more limited opportunities for working on language and socialization. James, Nellie, and every other child with Asperger's live with this catch-22, a reality in which their deficits deter them from the very life experiences they have dear and regular need for. It is their neurotypical siblings and peers who get invited to parties, who are called and buddied up to, who forever have the chance to interact not just with success but with a continual next chance to just keep getting better at it (socializing, that is).

Fourth, in an awful and painful reality that's often overlooked, the child with Asperger's goes through her days and nights without the understanding, admiring, accepting, and so on that other children know routinely. The fact is that such a child is less easy to grasp, understand, and relate to, not just by children, but even by the adults in their lives at home and school. When it comes to understanding another person, love is not enough. Many loving parents' hearts break continually at their own sense of not being able to somehow resonate with their child the way they would wish and maybe as they resonate with their other children or even children who are not their own.

How serious is a child's not getting enough understanding and acceptance? I compare it to a plant not getting enough water and sunshine. I have yet to meet one child with Asperger's who does not want more understanding, and who does not like being understood. But what choice and say do they have in this matter? And so again, *the worlds they create, if nothing else, help children with Asperger's to replenish and sustain themselves in a world that can be so unintentionally neglecting, hurtful, threatening, and unresponsive.*

In addition, the child with Asperger's often has learning issues, anxiety and depression, sensory sensitivities, and so on, difficulties that in themselves can hamper one's existence. But that is hardly all that the child with Asperger syndrome contends with.

Just because children are born with Asperger neurology does not give them a free pass from the trials and tribulations of life and growing up. Children with Asperger's have to navigate all the developmental transitions and tasks that neurotypical children face. They have to separate and individuate, develop life skills, and negotiate the perils of adolescence and an oncoming adulthood, including their sexuality. Children with Asperger's are in no way immune from catastrophic illness (their own or loved ones'), trauma, abuse, accidents, poverty, broken families, on and on.

The slings and arrows of life fall just as heavy on children with Asperger's, probably heavier. Because of their neurological makeup, children with Asperger's are more likely to suffer the ill-effects of untoward events and circumstances. Lacking the resources of greater self-understanding and the protective buffering and support of social connection, such children are more susceptible to the stresses and strains of life's miseries due, for example, to their parents' marital strife or loss of a loved one.

The leaden backpacks that we watch middle-schoolers bend under the weight of are mere bags of eider down compared to the inestimable baggage that the child with Asperger's lugs and lives under every moment of every day. As the parent or teacher of such a child, you know well that burden too. For you see it, sense it, maybe feel it too, and wish more than anything that you might find ways to lighten it.

2

THE CHILD'S VIEW

Asperger syndrome has an objective existence, in just the way that a table and snow do. Though I thoroughly appreciate debates as to what makes for normalcy—and, again, we'll get to them in due time—it is not a question of relativity or philosophy as to whether children with Asperger syndrome frequently experience certain hallmark traits due to neurological differences. *They do.*

That more objective existence, at least in the world of psychiatry and mental health, is officially embodied in the diagnostic entity *Asperger Disorder* as included in the *Diagnostic and Statistical Manual of Mental Disorders* (DSM-IV-TR 2000), the reference manual used by clinicians to make psychiatric diagnoses. That official diagnostic entity lists specific aspects of an "impairment in social interaction" as well as "repetitive and stereotyped patterns of behavior, interests, and activities" (pp.63–64).

These diagnostic criteria are worthy and have their place. They inform clinicians, sharpen diagnosis, and reduce the large numbers of children with Asperger's who go undetected and untreated. By enhancing diagnosis these criteria help get children to the right treatments quicker. The enhanced communication that can result between clinicians, allied therapists, and educators also has obvious benefits for the child. And some would argue that, most critical of all; a well-defined diagnostic disorder permits researchers to work toward better understanding and treatments.

When the DSM committee meets to debate and decide on new diagnoses, they seek validity and consensus. By *validity*, I mean they strive to identify the traits and behaviors most consistent with and distinctive for a specific disorder. By *consensus*, I mean that they strive to denote the clinical data—behaviors, traits, and so forth—that a majority of reasonable clinicians can see and agree upon. In coming to their difficult decisions, the DSM committee is guided by the ideal that their diagnostic criteria reflect the *objective* Truth of external reality. The assumption is that the diagnostic definition of Asperger's equals what the disorder actually looks like in a real child.

For all its undeniable power and utility, however, what does the Asperger diagnosis tell us in the full, rich and immediate sense of who a child is? Do those stilted phrases full of clinical jargon convey the being of the child with Asperger's that you love and care for, that you know and educate? To really know a child with Asperger's we can't rely on observations from a distance. We need to get up close, very close.

Though it may sound like bad science to say this, parents and teachers cannot depend on the *DSM-IV-TR*'s objective data to enlighten them or tell them everything. When coming to know the child with Asperger's who lives with you or who sits in your classroom, you are going to need *subjective* data that, make no mistake about it, holds relevance, import, and truth to rival anything to be found in the *DSM-IV-TR* or any other psychiatric handbook or journal.

Knowing a child with Asperger's requires that you climb into the Asperger experience. Think of aspiring students who go abroad to immerse themselves in a foreign culture and language. In order to grasp the child's daily experience and life in a real and palpable way, you need, as much as you can, to see through the child's eyes, hear through her ears, feel through her skin, and think through her brain. Of course, you can't actually put yourself in the child's brain. But you can come to know such a child very, very well, and in ways that will wholly transform your relationship and effectiveness with her. To get what I mean, we will take a quick trip through the possible world of experience that the child with Asperger's lives in.

Let's start with the sensory sensitivity that often comes along with Asperger's. Diagnostic manuals can define the criteria, journals of autism can document the percentage of children who have it, and medical research can examine the neurophysiology that accounts for it. But how much does that information itself help the actual child? And, just as critical to ask, how much does that help you, the parent or teacher who is trying to help that child?

To do something constructive for the child, meaning to make the moment easier for the child and to foster growth in this area—a dual-pronged goal that, whatever the behavior or experience, we will ever keep our eyes on—demands that we know something more specific. By specific, I don't mean knowing the precise milliampere threshold at which an olfactory nerve cell in the nose fires. I mean something plainer that usually lies in front of, and not inside, our own bystanders' noses. The most relevant question for parents and teachers does not concern itself with the underlying chemistry of smell or sight. The most relevant question is how does one particular child experience that particular sensory sensitivity? For you to relate to and understand the child or pupil before you, the central question becomes: *What*, for him or her, *must that feel like?*

Reflect on your own experiences. Have you ever been stuck in traffic on a hot and smelly bus for many hours? Have you ever been unable to sleep or focus because of the construction crew down the street or the pounding bass from an all-night party in the apartment below? Have you ever driven for an extended time straight into solar glare or conducted a long telephone call with someone who spoke very loudly? Whoever you are, I am sure you've had your share of sensory discomfort. For most of us, however, the duress is mild, short-lived, and infrequent. What's more, when we are bothered sensorily, we usually can do something about it. Our complaints, moreover, stand a good chance of getting other people's attention, sympathy, and even response.

Now, imagine that your encounters with sensory overload came daily, or hourly, or by the minute. Magnify the intensity ten- or a hundred-fold. My comparison is not excessive. If they were able and willing, many children with Asperger's would tell you that it's worse than how I'm putting it. Imagine that your daily environment assaulted you with sounds, lights, feelings, smells, and sights that made your home sweet home, school, or clinic office unbearably noxious *to you*. Imagine that you had to live in and couldn't escape environments in which you perpetually felt sensory discomfort and distress. How long do you suppose you could take it?

Then there is the loneliness. To grasp what this can mean for the child with Asperger's, you have to forget any notions you hold that the child wants it that way. We all know for certain that the child with Asperger's has social awkwardness and difficulties that can wreak havoc in her life. New research is showing that children with Asperger's seek friendships and connections much more than was credited. They are better at it, too, than we realized. This encouraging data, however, doesn't undo the social frustrations, rejections, failures, humiliations, anxieties, on and on, that pervade the social existence of these children. Even when the child seeks companionship, her best efforts run a good chance of not working. While some of her aloneness may represent choice and temperament, it also can represent protective adaptation against a social world that looms hard, painful and unattainable.

Feelings are another major problem area for children with Asperger's. Do we need a self-reference to better understand? Try summoning a recent moment when feelings, any feelings, near overwhelmed you. It can be awful. That sense of disintegration or irritability, which may occasionally trouble us, can resemble life as usual for the child with Asperger's. By way of their neurology, these children are often delayed in their ability to know and express what they feel. Those deficits make the child vulnerable to constant feelings of confusion, vague overexcitement, and unclear emotional states that threaten to overwhelm their overstimulated bodies. Tics and other signs of excessive body tension tend to plague these children.

Do you have the capacity to soothe yourself? That is a psychological luxury that few children with Asperger's enjoy. They have many fewer and smaller resources to self-regulate and buttress themselves against the emotional vagaries and storms of life. Add to this painful and stressful mix, the clinical anxiety and depression that commonly accompanies Asperger's. The child with Asperger's typically lacks the social connections and friendships that can serve to counteract and protect against stress and distress. This disadvantage makes the child more susceptible to emotional suffering and the behavioral consequences that follow. As a result, children with Asperger's know more than their fair share of impulsivity, anger, moodiness, and aggression, including self-injury and suicide.

We once believed that the Earth, and not the Sun, was the center of our universe. That earlier misperception was based largely on a lack of astronomical science, an error that Copernicus corrected. That is not my point, however. Our earlier belief in an Earth-centered galaxy arose from our human tendency to see ourselves and world as the ultimate nucleus of everything. Earth was ours, went the hubris of our thinking, and so how could anything but our planet be at the center and core of it all? While that kind of self-centered thinking makes for poor science, it can help us to discover good psychology, especially good psychology pertaining to the child with Asperger's.

Anyone who hopes to reach and affect the child with Asperger's needs to redraw their map of the solar system, putting the child at its absolute center *for that is exactly how the child experiences his life.* (This, you probably are already catching on, applies to all children, whether neurotypical, having Asperger's, or having any other difficulty.)

Trying to enter into a child's experience is not, by the way, the same as being sympathetic to the child. We can sympathize with a child and her predicament without feeling or knowing that experience. It is also not the same as pity, of course, or feeling bad for a child's circumstances or experiences. Taking a child's perspective, walking in his shoes, is a good start though that understanding can be mostly intellectual and lack the emotional getting of what a child feels or experiences. It is a rich mix of cognitive, emotional, and experiential understanding that I refer to.

So, in fact, how does a parent or teacher come to know a child's experience, come to know what having Asperger's means and is felt like by an actual child?

- How is it that we can know what other neurotypical people in our lives experience? How, for example, do you know what your other children, spouse or partner think and feel? One obvious way is that they tell you, and you listen. Because of its repetition or manner of delivery, it can be easy or become reflexive to dismiss what the child with Asperger's tells you as somehow carrying less meaning or significance. Listen for what the child is trying to convey, and make sure you get it.

- Ask or nudge, just as you do with others. "What'd you think of that soup?" "Is the air conditioner too cold?" "Do you like the perfume I wear or does it bother your sense of smell?" Check in with the child.

- Observe closely. Sometimes we know what other people feel by watching them. We notice the catch in their voice, the teary eye, the blushed cheek.

Children with Asperger's show the same kinds of reactions. Sometimes, Asperger-like tics and mannerisms exacerbate when the child is somehow stressed, and lessen when the child is somehow comfortable. Use these continuous nonverbal cues as telling signals of what the child is experiencing.

• Keep in mind that trying to step into the child-centric view of the child with Asperger's is not distinct from how you do it for other children and people. It, however, seems to be a necessity for the child with Asperger's since her innately neurological being may make her sharing herself more difficult with others, even with parents and teachers.

• Just take it in. While the understanding and insights you glean will make it easier to be and interact with the child, you need not always or even mostly transform this data into action. Your simply getting it will be noticed and registered by the child. What you learn will also inform how you yourself behave. If, for instance, the child with Asperger's takes a step back whenever you take a step forward, this might tell you to stay put, or even to take a small step back. This enhanced responsiveness on your part can, in turn, lead to the child's feeling safer, more understood, and closer to you.

• Be a good explorer. *Just taking it in* can sound rather passive, and some people have trouble with not doing. But being a good watcher and listener is actually a very active and demanding endeavor. Think of a loud tourist quickly traipsing through the jungle. Smart and wary animals will run and hide. But if the explorer sits still and is patient, she'll soon see and hear all kinds of wildlife and wonders. Create the conditions and attitude in you to be open to the child with Asperger's. Prepare to receive as much as to do.

- Lay aside preconceived notions. You know a lot about Asperger syndrome in its official and objective terms. Forget stereotypes and definitions of the disorder. Study the child you are with as if a new species, and see what she teaches you about herself and her experience, what she shows you about her Asperger's—in many ways, the only Asperger's that matters.

- Develop your own database derived from your own eyes, ears, and so forth. Though he cannot articulate it as such, your child or student is the real expert on what it is like to have and live with Asperger's. You have the absolute best teacher if you are willing to learn from him.

- Be wary of too quickly writing off any behavior, comment, symptom, or experience as the "static" of Asperger's. To do so will surely lead you to miss out on much and will compromise your relationship with the child. Think of yourself as a detective whose job it is to decipher the meanings and good reasons behind the child's behaviors and words. This, be sure, does not mean ignoring the neurological reality of Asperger's. It means realizing that the child, being human, cannot help but develop a self and ways in response to that Asperger's. It is this human dialectic between the neurology and the child—unique for every child—that you wish to grow increasingly curious, aware, and understanding of.

3

THE PARENT'S VIEW

I typically find writing about parents to be a delicate subject. I say this as both a psychologist and a parent. No one loves the child or understands him more than the parent. How pretentious, so it seems, for others, such as myself, to intrude into that primary relationship. Writing about a matter and children, in some ways, so sensitive and vulnerable, so misunderstood, seems to heighten the challenge. And so I venture forth asking parent readers for their leniency now and throughout the book for the inevitable moments when I overstep, insult, or otherwise miss my mark of writing a book that supports and enlightens parents.

As I just alluded to, the majority of parents have gotten to this point in time having been through some kind of journey. Some parents will have heard the diagnosis of Asperger's early in the process. Their experience with clinicians and schools may have run a smooth and direct course, having gotten their child all the right services and timely too. These parents may have encountered "help" that's welcoming, responsive, competent, knowledgable, and that really is helpful. In my experience, this heartwarming tale does not tell about a majority of parents whose children have Asperger's. The parents I've met or hear about too frequently have traveled a more circuitous route full of detours and delays.

To say that you, the parent, are the expert on his or her child is true, and yet this statement needs qualifying. Parents are often not educators and usually are not mental health clinicians. (Though, of course, some parents of children with Asperger's are.) Once they hear the term Asperger's, parents are prone to learn a lot more from clinicians, educational specialists, and from their own reading of the solid literature that is out there in bookstores for parents to read on the subject.

Some of what these books and experts tell parents synchronizes beautifully; sometimes it clashes. What are parents to believe? What methods do they pursue? Which clinicians and clinics do they sign up with? Which schools do they enroll their child in, or, maybe, the question is what services do they request or advocate for? I imagine that every parent of a child with Asperger's wishes they had a crystal ball which could, not tell the future, but tell them which school, program, method, teacher, therapist …[fill in the blank]…can most help their child realize all she or he can be. That, of course, is a dream that all parents of all children can relate to. The stakes, and perils, though, for the child with Asperger's are steeper and greater.

The overall approach, and specific strategies, mentioned in this book will in no way replace all of the good data and learning that parents have gotten to this day. I will not advise you as to which educational program to pursue or what kind of school environment will suit your child best. The truth is there is no way I could know that. Nor can I say a few words or even offer up a psychological program that will utterly clarify your own thinking on the diagnosis and your child. It is far too complicated for me or that. What I can do, however, is help you to find a new balance and a new vantage from which to encounter your child, a new way of seeing her or him—a way, even if closely familiar to what has been, that opens you to new possibilities, hopefulness, and understanding.

Prior to it touching your own life, like many parents, you well may have known little about Asperger's. In fact, you may never have even heard the word. Many of the parents I've met had, however, heard the word *autism*, and that association, when mentioned in relation to their own child, near always felt like a kick to the head and the gut, delivering a discouraging and fearful shock to their lives and, at the bottom line, breaking their heart. Whatever way that the eventual diagnosis and news got to you, it is now done, ancient history. I do not mean that how you reacted and still feel about the diagnosis doesn't matter, for it does—*essentially* so. All you can do is to go from this day on, putting the diagnosis into a place and context that comfortably works with and alongside you as you learn and do all you can to maximize your child's growth and development. These words and goal might sound trite for their obviousness, and yet they are true and lie at the heart of this book and my approach.

To bring my hifalutin talk down to earth and your home, shift your attention for the moment to a window box of flowers. Unfortunately, you do not know what kind of flowers you have, nor can anyone tell you. You know flowers need water and sunshine, but different flowers need different amounts of each. You don't know if your flower needs acidic or basic soil, what kinds of nutrients, on and on. I could belabor this example but you get the point, I think. At some point, your flower's survival depends on your becoming the expert. And how do you do that?

By studying books on agriculture, attaining a graduate degree in botany, by taking workshops on perennials, or maybe apprenticing at your local nursery? That would all teach you a lot. But would it help you to keep the flowers alive and blooming? No, the surest way would be a careful and observant method of trial and error, watching just what your gardening (i.e. experimental intervening) does to either promote or hamper your flowers' wellbeing. It might take some time, but eventually, you will be the world's expert on *your* flowers. (Some might jump in to say that that is exactly what good developmental and scientific research aims to do for children with Asperger's; and I would be the first to agree. But I am talking about more than just methods here and, again, I am not suggesting my approach as a substitute to any educational or therapy program that's been shown to help.)

Even with all of the uncertainty, even in a sea of experts or among a team of professionals, you the parent can be the expert on your child. You can be the one who knows her best, who understands what she is communicating, what she wants and needs, and so forth. It demands a lot of a parent. It demands your taking in what others say and recommend. It demands you heeding the wisdom of educators and clinicians while balancing that with your own sense and understanding of your child. It demands your weighing the evidence with your own experiences with your child. It demands your regularly wiping your glasses to see your child more clearly, as he or she is, as she or he is trying to show you.

I fear that this might sound like "touchy-feely" psychobabble or gobbledygook. It is true that I am exalting the ideal of the child with Asperger's being desperately needing and eminently worthy of our appreciation, meaning appreciation for what goes on inside their heads, hearts, and everywhere between. But what I am saying is not nonsense or the theoretical poppycock of a therapist who only wishes it were so. This is the truth that children with Asperger's have taught me day in day out for more than a quarter of a century.

What can your child teach you the parent?

- Wipe the slate clean. This is not a call to forget what you've learned or experienced, or what you know to be true. It means open yourself to new ideas, new ways of seeing your child, and new ways of thinking about Asperger's as it affects your child.

- Sidestep conceptions of bad or good children. Likewise, do not think in terms of broken or sick children. Think, *this is my child* and *she can show me her way* of thinking, feeling, playing, communicating, and so on. Get to know your own flower of a child as well as you can.

- Turn away from naysaying and dour predictions. I have worked with many parents whose children totally smashed through the glass ceilings supposed experts in autism had set for their children at a fairly young age. While thoroughly unrealistic expectations that ignore who a child is can be destructive, so can expectations that are grossly limited, underwhelming, or ignore the child's demonstrated capacity to grow.

- Keep keeping at it. Everything good you put into the child today will eventually show its benefits in the future. If the child grows a tiny bit today, there is every reason to assume that the child will grow a tiny bit—or even more—on the next day, and the next. There is every reason to ever seek greater understanding to support your child's maturing and connecting.

- Experiment. True, our children are not laboratory hamsters. But trial and error, seeing in careful and small doses what kinds of experience and interactions help your child, is a great way of learning what works and what does not. You do not need an expensive assessment test or a doctorate in psychology to figure out, for instance, that your reggae music in the background seems to settle your child or that she listens to you best when you speak quietly.

- Detoxify your frustration. Parents know so much frustration, especially when they cannot do or accomplish all that they wish they might for their child. Frustration can get in the way of seeing your child clearly, of understanding, of working with teachers, and at being the kind of presence you want to be and that can best connect with your child. Find active and reliable ways—talking with trusted family, friends, or counsellors—to deal with frustration.

- Celebrate baby steps. Development occurs as grass grows, too slowly to see. Waiting and looking for major leaps in development will frustrate you and your child and, paradoxically, will deter growing. Train yourself to notice near imperceptible improvements, and allow yourself to take joy and pride in this movement forward. When taken one after another, baby steps can eventually get you and your child to places you never imagined reaching.

- Keep your responsibilities clear. As a parent you do not have the responsibility of making everything okay, of restoring what is done and can't be changed, or of being a 200-percent überParent. You are just a parent who happens to have a child with Asperger's. It is that complex and that simple. All you bear the responsibility for is to ever strive to understand your child better, and the rest will follow.

- Tend to your tool box. As a psychologist who also has renovated two homes, I am not a big fan of comparing life skills to tools. But it does convey the message. Parenting is a set of skills that few parents come to naturally, but that most parents can get even better at. Try to mix up your use of tools and broaden your repertoire daily. Avoid stagnancy or using the same old trick for everything. It will grow old and ineffective.

- Know when to take a break. You cannot make good things happen every minute of every day. You—like your child—will have some bad days as a parent; some days you would have been ahead by just staying in bed with the covers pulled over your head. When all is going badly, and when nothing seems to be working, give yourself and your child a break from you and your best efforts. Parenting any child, with or without Asperger's, is a marathon not a sprint. There is always tomorrow.

- Your parenting matters—*a lot!* We barely survived the old and malignant deception that parents cause autism and Asperger's. No parent has that power. Asperger's is due to neurology, period. But that doesn't mean that your parenting of your child with Asperger's is any less relevant, for good or bad, than your parenting is for a child who doesn't have Asperger's. Your parenting can profoundly influence your child's growth, adjustment, and sense of self.

4

THE TEACHER'S VIEW

There is much to compare between parents and teachers when it comes to children with Asperger syndrome, and, for sure, what I suggest for one can well apply to the other. Both care deeply about the child. Though not the child's parent, many teachers feel love for the students they educate. Both parents and teachers want to move the child ahead developmentally. They want to see him connected, especially with peers, and connected too, with themselves (the parent or teacher). Teachers and parents also share the same frustrations in dealing with children that they somehow just don't feel they reach or help the way they would like. Like parents, teachers can know many moments when they feel confused, disconnected, and unsure of what they are doing as well as longer moments when they might even question whether what they do matters, whether it actually helps. Such reactions can be natural byproducts of caring and working with such children. To hope and strive in any endeavor implies that doubt and discouragement will be there too.

There are clear distinctions between parents and the teacher also. Parents generally live with their child whereas the teacher has the child for more limited and well-designated times. While parents hope to impart many influences that resemble and overlap if not, at times, duplicate the functions of the teacher, the teacher's role with the child tends to be more sharply defined, limited, structured, and articulated.

The teacher's job is to teach the child with Asperger's. The subject matter might be reading, language arts, or mathematics. It can be history, a foreign language, science, physical education, or music. The instruction might take place in a regular classroom or in a classroom for special education. The instruction can be across an entire classroom or occur through one-on-one tutoring. While the teaching tends to address concrete academic subjects appropriate to the child's level of ability and achievement, the goal is to impart knowledge, facts, and learning skills by whatever means can further that noble and necessary purpose. With the greater awareness and attention being paid to these children by school systems, teacher and "classrooms" are increasingly being targeted at neurologically based deficits, such as those in speech and language and social pragmatics. These interventions likely involve other children and can even take place in the cafeteria or on the playground, that is—where children in school naturally reside and interact.

Whatever the subject, mission, or setting of the learning doesn't much matter, at least, not in what I am about to say. Somehow, *the teacher needs to reach the child with Asperger's.* Without some kind of connection, the learning will be stunted. As I'll soon describe, that connection may not at all look like the connection that teachers are taught to seek and make. And yet the child knows when he or she has been reached in that way, and the teacher will know it too. It is through that relationship, that ever-growing state of connection and comfort with the teacher and the learning environment, that the child is most open to receiving, processing, and learning, whatever the subject or task.

What does such a state of connectedness between child and teacher look like? As I just suggested above, giving this question the attention it deserves may require teachers to ponder what their ideal teaching connections with neurotypical children look like.

If teachers are like the rest of us—and we know they are exactly that, only with added knowledge and skills—they enjoy that feeling of reaching the child. That experience can show itself in many overtly behavioral ways. The child tells the teacher of her affection or liking, or the child shows it by smiling at the teacher or showing interest and effort. The teacher may feel that positive regard or connection in the child's getting with the program, meaning that the child owns and performs the role of the good student by behaving, studying, and being a good school citizen. A child may spontaneously say that she enjoyed a lesson or directly answer in the affirmative when her teacher asks. It is easy for non-educators to grasp how cooperative and successful learners can foster a sense of connection in their teachers.

Teachers, however, also know how to reach less eager and less model students. They know how to foster *and* recognize signs of connection even when a child is reluctant, distracted, unmotivated, or oppositional, a challenge that to the noneducator rest of us can look to be near impossible. Teachers are experts in channeling their creativity and humanness to find places of connection, for they know that without those junctions they will have much less influence with the child. Hard as that task may be, teachers also know the enormous satisfaction and reward of reaching the child who does not come to school eager to learn and engage.

The child with Asperger's can, however, present even a highly experienced and skilled teacher with a new kind of dilemma. Though many children with Asperger's are willing and easy pupils, many are not. Children with Asperger's can be eccentric, preoccupied (with their interests), uninterested (in the teacher's interests, that is, the matter being taught), unmotivated (to learn that material and knowledge), and seem unrelentingly impervious (to the teacher's best attempts to get through). They can be disruptive and show little investment in or response to methods or strategies that work with neurotypical children. Likewise, they may have little wish to please their teachers or win their approval, or so it can appear. Many of these children appear to have little need to share their thoughts, experiences, feelings, and reactions with others, which may include the teacher. I am sure that both teacher and parent readers could add much here, to detail the ways in which the specific children with Asperger's whom they know can resist and derail the educational process and its agents.

I suppose that some could argue the case that teaching does not always require that a relationship is formed, that learning can occur in a more objective and less interpersonally bound context. In fact, some might suggest that the case for children with Asperger's is even stronger. Don't many of these children, for example, learn well, some best, simply by reading books or pursuing information on their own? Isn't a neutral nonperson-mediated form of learning their preferred medium anyway?

While these are fair questions and reasonable observations based in some reality, my long experience of knowing children with Asperger's tells me that the truth is more complex and less visible to the eyes and ears. These children want to connect, be reached, and share, *in their ways*—ways, to be sure, that may look very distinct from the ways we are used to.

On average, research shows, teachers are extremely reliable and accurate observers of their students. Year after year, eventually over decades, teachers amass a sizable and impressive database of children they have taught or who they've known running on their playgrounds and walking through their hallways. This is the personal reference that teachers use almost automatically to meet, assess, and (know how to) work with various students. That mounting experience with former students is the powerful lens through which teachers greet and view the new students who enter their classrooms each fall.

The child with Asperger's may not fit this template. He may not resemble any child that the teacher has known before, and, as teachers tell me can happen, he may seem not to respond to any of the strategies or styles of teaching that have, in that one educator's years of teaching, previously proved effective.

Am I now able to fill this gap and tell you, the teacher, how to see this child or what to do with him? You can already anticipate my answer to the contrary. I cannot. But I am certain that you, the teacher, will be soon be able to do that yourself.

- Sign up for a course taught by the child. What I mean is, let this child be your teacher. For a bit of time, lay aside all that you know about neurotypical children and all of the children you have taught well. If you allow—by actively listening and observing—the child with Asperger's will show you who she is, how she works, what she needs, and all that relevant information.

- Don't take it personally. A child with Asperger's can frustrate others, and that may include her teachers. Try—and this can be hard—to not take the child's way of being with you as a referendum of you as either a teacher or a person, or as a professional who is supposed to know how to reach such a child. Instead, see it as part of Asperger's and a reasonable aspect of her having to cope with a life that, given her neurological difficulties, can be difficult.

- Be a detective. The child's behaviors or ways are not so much bad or good, as they are simply her ways of being, ways that may have everything to do with having Asperger's. Rather than critique these off-putting ways or dismiss them as just the unavoidable stuff of Asperger's, try to learn more about them. When do they worsen or lessen, what seems to exacerbate them, and what that you do as teacher seems to attract or repel the child? Good reasons often lie behind the child's words and actions. Maybe you can identify them.

- Be hopeful. As I said in the last chapter, many parents have endured the despair of hearing experts tell them how their child will developmentally fail. Those days are, fortunately, mostly gone. Be encouraging, not unrealistically, but in the sense that you, and the team, ever keep helping the child move ahead to a future whose limits are not yet known.

- Experiment. Akin to the current "Response to Intervention" movement in education, try different approaches with the child. If you have a hunch that the child will learn better in that comfortable chair in the corner, give it a trial. If—contrary to what has been going on and despite the child's mediocre efforts—you wonder if the child would engage better with more advanced reading material, give it a whirl for a day or two. If you see tiny movement, give it a few more days. What have you got to lose?

- Take counsel. Teaching these children can be trying and frustrating, and confront you with a challenge that your education and experience feels not to have prepared you for. Talk about your experiences and ideas with colleagues or others that you trust. This can help prevent your frustration from obstructing your purview, teaching, and interactions with the child.

- Educate yourself. Take advantage of workshops, conferences, books, and any other media that can offer you some information, method, or confirmation of your work with these children. When we do not feel that we understand what's going on in our work, when we feel unsuccessful or helpless, that is when we're most vulnerable to stress and burnout.

- Recalibrate your growth ruler. The criteria and accomplishments that you are accustomed to seeing and registering may not apply as well to the child before you. You may need to readjust your scale of assessment to detect gains that are smaller and that come more slowly. Allow yourself to take pride and joy in these modest steps ahead, and to help the child see that you recognize his efforts and their value.

- Heed your feelings. If you are feeling especially frustrated with a child, do not ignore it. If you dislike a child, or are dreading your class with him each day, or feeling guilty over not reaching him more, take that signal seriously. Do whatever it takes—counsel, consultation, a break—to come to understand and grow past these stressful feelings. The goal is not just to get past the hour or through the day; it is to find more lasting resolution and comfort in the work with such children over the long run.

- Put yourself on a pedestal. I am not suggesting you grow a big head or see yourself as some deity of an educator to be worshipped. I mean try to remind yourself of how important you can be in the child's school day, learning, and life. Though the child may not show it in any way you yet recognize, you may be very special in his heart and mind, and in ways that he is unable to show you more directly or understandably. Assume that the child wants to find some comfortable way of being with you, and work to help the child and you establish that space together.

- Think relatedness. Even as you strive to teach the child algebra, French, or language arts, keep the child's connection to you in mind. The child who feels connected with the teacher will work harder, be more open and available, and learn better.

- Seek understanding. The more and better you understand the child before you, your own teaching self in relation to that child, and your shared work, the more successful you will be. And, though each child with Asperger's differs from every other child with Asperger's, your growing more able and willing to know one such child will generalize, so that getting to know the next child, and then the next, will come quicker, more easily, and with less frustration.

5

CREATING A
SAFE PLACE

The notion of a safe place for the child with Asperger's to be may strike some readers as almost too obvious to state, no less focus a chapter on. And it is quite likely that the child you parent or teach has the good fortune of knowing such a good place under your caring watch and powers. Unfortunately, not all children with Asperger's have such a place, especially as they go through their days, or have one that is less safe than is to be desired and less than the child requires. Though it is for those children that this chapter is most dedicated, the matter and strategies discussed can help all parents and educators think about the issue of "a safe place" for the child with Asperger's, when he is with you and when he is not.

The dictionary defines *safety* as "the condition of being safe from undergoing or causing hurt, injury or loss" (Merriam-Webster 1998). What exactly do I mean by "a safe place" when speaking about children with Asperger's? In part I mean just what the dictionary says, that in a safe place the child with Asperger's is free from physical harm. This implies that in addition to not hurting the child themselves, parents and teachers will protect him from harm dealt by others. Others, we suppose, would include other children too. But safety includes a lot more, especially for a child, and yet more so for a child with Asperger's.

A safe place, for the child with Asperger's, might be a place that is sensorily comfortable or at least tolerable. As you know as well as I, children with Asperger's often have exquisite sensitivities to sensory stimuli. A safe place, to such a child, neither overwhelms nor assaults her sensory sensitivities. (Chapter 7 addresses sensory issues in detail and explores their realities at home and school, along with strategies to manage them.) Suffice it to say for now that much of the school environment can inherently over-arouse a child with Asperger's. Consider, for instance, the average sensory stimuli of a school cafeteria—with its overhead fluorescent lights, strong food smells, and chaotic rush of children moving and talking. That multi-sensory admixture of stimuli can make a child with Asperger's ill at ease, and, if the stimuli continue, keep him in that state. Depending on the stimuli and the child, that state of sensory arousal can range from mere and negligible irritation to a full-blown overload and shut-down. Again, throughout the book we'll discuss ways to make home and school a safer place. For now, our simpler goal is to appreciate the child's experience, in this case, his sensory experience of the environment where he or lives or is schooled, an experience that might be far less than optimal or agreeable.

A safe place can mean a place where the child feels sheltered from social ostracizing or verbal teasing. The social milieu of a school can be a rough and ready place for the child whose abilities to interact and chat it up on the playground are no match for his peers. A safe place might equally be a place that not only shelters him, but that somehow shelters others by not allowing him, the child with Asperger's, to tease or mistreat others. In other words, it can feel safe for a child to be with an adult, parent or teacher, who—by maintaining structure, providing oversight, socially facilitating, and so forth— helps the child avoid social scratches and fender benders, if not total collisions. Such damage control can be a viable piece of the child's guided social life, one that provides a substantial sense of safety.

What makes for a safe place for the child with Asperger's can also take the form of what we might consider to be more psychological reasons. They could, just as well and accurately and with much less ado, be called human reasons having to do with finding a place that lets the children be who they are. Let me explain, by using an example that the rest of us who do not have Asperger's can maybe relate to.

Compare two social events to which you're invited. One is a formal affair, a dinner party requiring fancy dress, conversation with strangers, top-notch etiquette, and all that jazz. If you are like me, such an occasion is rare, and when you leave, even if walking out into a frigid New England evening, you are relieved to be out. You loosen your tie and collar, take a deep breath, and thank goodness that as far as you know, you won't be doing this again for a long time.

Now compare with that an evening that many more of us know on a more frequent basis. Your good friends come over for take-out. You are tired from a hard week and, being utterly at ease with your long-time friends, you don't even plan what kind of take-out it will be. It will be decided when they get here. You know with these friends that you can wear a flannel shirt and jeans, watch the game if you like, make your lame jokes, drink a bit too much, or not even sound too intelligent.

You get the point. And how does it feel? Your two-and-a-half hours in tails—despite the fine food and surroundings—seem like a weekend, whereas the five hours with your friends speed by and the evening is called only because you are all falling asleep on the couch, it being a late Friday after a long week. How do you compare the safety you feel with your friends versus that other experience?

A second example will illustrate my idea more vividly. Imagine how you feel with someone with whom you feel little personal comfort, perhaps a relative you feel is critical of you or a boss who annoys you or worse. Now imagine, instead, a beloved family member or old friend with whom you feel the ultimate safety. Can you identify what it is that makes for the difference? It probably involves some good measure of acceptance, a sense that who you are, warts and all, is someone that that the Other is okay with, or maybe even likes and loves. Maybe it's the way you laugh too loud or the way you spill your coffee or the way you drive a bit unevenly. Whatever your failings, that other person seems not to mind, not even notice. They are too busy, so it appears, relating to and being with you.

So, what is the equivalent of that kind of safe place when speaking about the child with Asperger's, your child or your pupil? A safe place is a place where the child feels to some degree, if not wholly, that his or her being is okay, adequate, and enough. How does a parent or teacher convey that kind of respect and regard?

By dropping heaps of verbal praise, of words that say *we like you just the way you are*? By awarding gold plastic trophies and blue ribbons that say "Good Job" and "No. 1"? By offering heartfelt and eloquent explanations that "in this house or this classroom, you are accepted"? Well, I'm not going to say that these are wrongheaded or that the child doesn't get something good out of them. They can be useful. But on average, it is not shiny props or gracious words that will win the day and win over the children, that will convince them *deep down inside where it counts* that they are welcome just as they are. Trite as it may sound, the only thing that will persuade children of their acceptance—that this is a safe place where they can be and maybe even blossom—will be parents' and teachers' actual acceptance, their genuinely meaning and showing it.

- Take the child's perspective. While you will use your grownup knowledge and sense of what a safe place means, it is the child's version that matters. You, as a silly example, may keep out tigers and snakes, but if the child fears puppies and snails (and you do not keep *them* out), the child will feel neither safe nor protected.

- Preserve safety first. Whatever a parent or teacher is trying to accomplish or teach, that lesson or moment will be compromised if the child doesn't feel safe. How well could you or I work at a task while feeling threatened by the environment, people, or most anything else? You cannot guarantee that the child will feel an enduring sense of security, and surely not all the time, but you can strive toward that end.

- Consider safety, in all its myriad forms and disguises. What, we try to ever seek and identify, are the things that threaten, unsettle, or irritate the child? Whether physical, psychological, emotional, environmental, social or whatever, experiencing greater safety around such stimuli can foster the child's knowing greater comfort. And, for the child with Asperger's, each molecule more of comfort and security is of value, and, in the long run, adds up to something substantial.

- Listen to the child. If she says that something bothers her, take it to heart and maybe action. If she asks a question about something, it probably matters to her (for it was on her mind). Don't shy away from asking the child what she thinks or feels about some aspect of the home or classroom, if you have a sense that it might be an issue *for her*.

- Watch the child. Language communication is always welcome. But many children, like adults, are not so willing or adept at putting their worries, fears, and even petty annoyances into words. We also need to welcome gestures and nonverbal communication for they are often a source of information. If the child holds her nose, well, that a smell is bugging her seems obvious. If she squints, the light might be in her eyes. Use your eyes and ears as fully as you can. They are powerful receivers.

- Go slowly. This is a suggestion that I will revisit again and again. When we, as parents or teachers, get too headstrong, focused, and driven, when we move too fast, we are prone to miss seeing and hearing, especially seeing and hearing smaller, quieter, and subtler things. Make time and space, not just to smell the flowers, but to smell (see, feel, and so forth) what may not be perceived as so sweet or inviting by the child.

- Try it. If you talk a bit loud, try a bit softer. If you move a bit fast, try a little slower. Observe what seems to bring the child comfort, and try doing more in that direction. Likewise, try doing less of—or taking action in the environment to correct—that which seems to irritate or somehow bother the child.

- Show you get it. This refers to one point that I will come back to frequently. In much of our communications, we do not expect others to change or immediately do what we ask. But we want acknowledgment that it is heard and matters. If the child with Asperger's somehow makes clear that he is uncomfortable (or feeling unsafe) with something, show that you get it. Nod in recognition, repeat the child's words, or say something like, "I know the cafeteria smells are strong for you. I wish there was something I could do about that for you." Like any of us, even when nothing can be done, the child will much appreciate your heartfelt—so we hope—confirmation, and will feel closer to you for having received it.

6

TREASURING PRECIOUS GOODS

When I was in elementary school, "Show and Tell" was part of the routine. As we probably all know, Show and Tell allows children the opportunity to stand in front of the class and show off or describe just about anything. What sorts of things do children show and tell about? Souvenirs from trips, dead and live insects, things they've built or drawn, pictures of pets, and so forth. Commonly, a child's wish to share the spotlight is so great that he will volunteer himself even when he has nothing (on his mind) to show off. Under the stare of classmates, and the threat of the teacher's good-natured hook, the child will grab anything to talk about: "My mom makes cookies." "I saw a dinosaur." "My belt is white."

Any bystander witnessing this classroom happening anywhere would see right through the nervous giggles and bravado. She'd need no advanced degree in education or psychology, or be a parent herself, to see what's going on. Whatever the prop, whether a shell from the beach or a lost tooth, that bystander would see that it was all about a child's best effort to appear special in the eyes of his classmates and teacher. The specialness and poignancy of what a child shows and tells near hits us on the head in these once-in-a-while classroom events. In reality, that dynamic represents a life experience that is ongoing for the child at school, at home, and everywhere in between.

If we need further evidence of the child's wish to be special, we need to go no farther than that same classroom. Stick around for a few hours, and watch the young children vie for attention. "Me. Me! ME!" Children's arms pop up like spring-loaded catapults when the teacher asks a question, any question, whether or not they know the answer. Come to think of it, arms forever go up, even when there is no question. *Look at me. Listen to me. Think of me.* We know that the classroom can represent a perfect extension and mirror of the child's wish for specialness at home with his parents. It is so business as usual for kindergarten teachers to be called "Mommy" that they come to neither react nor notice it.

Now, turn your attention to another child, one that could live with you and one that doesn't have Asperger's. Imagine, if you will, a child who has a strong need to be noticed by and share with the parent she adores (aka you). He ever brings you the drawings and crafts that he makes, wanting only for you to think it is the greatest work of art ever known—known, that is, since his last creation hours before. When he's built a house of blocks or a sand castle, something too big to carry, he calls your name or grabs your hand to drag you back to see what he's accomplished. With the apprehension of a writer showing his manuscript to his editor, the child waits and watches for your reaction. "Do you like it, Mommy?" "Do you love it, Daddy?" "Is it your favorite ever?" (We all know what word could easily substitute for *it*.) The child likewise wants—*needs*—for you to notice his squeaky clarinet playing, his gymnastic tumbling, and his picking up his own toys. It is almost as if his deed has not occurred until your witnessing endows it with legitimacy.

The child's wish for the parent's or teacher's acknowledgment doesn't end with the things he makes. He wants you to know when he's hungry or itchy, and when his feet fall asleep. He wants you to know when he's angry or frustrated or feeling mistreated. "That's not fair. You love Eric more!" He wants you to know when he's scared (at the dentist) and when he's proud (after going anyway). He wants you to know what he sees. "Look, a lady bug." Seeing a rainbow by himself doesn't cut it; he needs you to see it too, to certify his perception with your Good Parent's (or Teacher's) Seal of Approval. He wants you to see his adding three plus three just as he wants you to know what he dreamt the night before.

Consider this sad and true instance from a high school classroom. A bright and learning disabled teenager I once treated, taking a big chance, put his all into a several page interpretation of a poem. He put his heart into the paper and, while nervous about the grade, hoped most that his newfound effort and insights would please his teacher. He came to his following session devastated. His teacher had drawn large and bold red lines through his paper. She'd given him a poor grade, and told him that he'd completely missed the meaning of the poem. Though this boy appreciated my telling him that poems don't have correct answers, he couldn't shake the deepest message he took away. "Why doesn't she just tell me I'm a moron who shouldn't be alive?"

Everything a child feels, thinks, wonders, fears, says, draws, and does is a reflection of the child's being, the child's *is*. When any of us reject or dismiss any of that, we reject and dismiss the child himself.

I am sure you've noticed that I have yet to mention Asperger's in this discussion. And, I worry, some readers, knowing children with Asperger's who seem to have little need to share any experience with any adult, are wondering if I know what I'm talking about and whether, indeed, I know these children. Readers who hold such doubts have gotten ahead of me.

It is true that many children with Asperger's seem to have less of a wish to share what they think and feel with those they love and like. Some parents and teachers may actually have read what I wrote and thought sadly, "If only my child would run to me to share a flower, or a game of catch, or a worry—*or anything*." Many parents of children with Asperger's feel shut out from the inner experiences and worlds of the children they love and crave to know more and up closer.

In direct contrast to what conventional wisdom has told us, children with Asperger's want notice, acceptance, and confirmation—even when that want in no way appears to resemble the way in which neurotypical children share and reach out to others, especially their parents and teachers. Children with Asperger's have thoughts, feelings, worries, fantasies, disappointments, and other emotions just like the rest of us. They too have insides that are rich, complex, and worthy of our attention and heeding. They want those innards to be respected and affirmed despite the fact that they themselves can make it harder for parents and teachers to do so.

However the experience of such children is limited or altered by the realities of their Asperger neurology, isn't that experience still itself in need of our acceptance and validation? Don't the children at the least need our notice and confirming for what the Asperger experience is *for them*, for what limitations, hardships, and implications their neurological deficits impose upon their days and existence?

That what these children possess on both the outside and inside is to be cherished should be assumed by all of us as a fact of human nature and psychology. That some conventional bias had advised us to dismiss some of the child's being as the residue of bad neurology is, I think, to be taken warily. We should not need scientific evidence that children with Asperger's have insides that matter and carry meaning. We know it's fact, because we ever live and experience it firsthand ourselves. What makes the creations, experiences, and inner worlds of children with Asperger's special is nothing more or less than that it is their own, that *it is theirs*. And that is all the proof that any of us should require to treat the child and his precious goods with our utmost curiosity, respect, and care.

- Know the hard score. Children with Asperger's get so much less confirmation than do their neurotypical peers. This frequent and sorry state of affairs is not blameworthy or to be pinned on any of us. Even as we do our best to respond to this dilemma and the children's needs, it pays to stay sensitized to just how being so shortchanged on a daily basis is, for many such children, life as usual.

- Do your own survey. Go through a day paying attention to how often you share something with others, or your other children or pupils do the same. Compare that with what you observe for the child with Asperger's. Do you notice, can you detect, moments where the child before you seems to be making an appeal that goes awry or is ignored?

- Respect the neurology. Many children with Asperger's, by their very nature, often show much less want or need to bring others into their experience. Hans Asperger, the Viennese pediatrician who wrote about these children back in the 1940s, described these children as "closed books" hard to open and enter into. Many parents and teachers dream if only the child would run to them with open arms and selves. Reaching out to be rebuffed has to hurt, especially for a loving parent or teacher. That is the Asperger's, not you.

- Register your own reactions. While, as the previous paragraph suggests, it is good to not take it personally, thereby keeping your hurts and such from discoloring your interactions with the child, it is important for you to know your true feelings. They are not be squelched or denied, for they will eventually make themselves known, probably in ways that either stress you or deter your being with the child. Let yourself feel sad or resentful for the connection the child with Asperger's does not make with you. Let yourself feel envy for the parents or teachers who spend their days with children, perhaps, who give them more of that warm and fuzzy stuff. You are human, and cannot sometimes help but feel such loss or feel sad for yourself.

• Remember the child's dilemma. The neurological deficits of Asperger's can make it difficult for the child to bring her insides to the outside, to be heard and understood by another person. She may not herself know what she feels or what her reaction is, so that she does not have something solid in her own mind and conscious to express aloud to someone else. Given how awkward and unsuccessful communicating with others can be, the child is prone to grow more isolated and self-contained. If the child perceives her own thoughts to be strange or unwanted, she will yet have a greater incentive to keep herself to herself.

• Believe in meaning. Some suggest that children with Asperger's have less going on to share, and that some of what they think or say lacks meaning, that it is to be taken as random static due to Asperger neurology. Children with Asperger's have taught me that such thinking is perilous. Every human being must confront an existential reality, create their own connections, meanings, and identities. Without such meaning, and having them shared, we all would grow lost and vulnerable. We all seek to find and create meaning and cohesion in our experiences and ourselves. Children with Asperger's are no different, nor are the adults whom they grow into.

• Parse the child. I, of course, do not mean to dissect her cold or analytically. Take a bit of time to do nothing but watch her. Think about her experiences as she goes through the minutiae of her existence under your eyes. Study her body tension and movements, her comments, her habits, her interactions or lack thereof, and so forth, trying not to ignore or minimize the significance of any of it for her. Ideally, we want to get to know the child as intimately as we like to know ourselves.

- Seek moments of cherishing. I am not suggesting a veritable love-fest or that either parent or teacher should be spending constant effort and time "beholding" the child. That would be as undoable as it would be unhelpful (and, probably, unwanted by the child herself). I am instead envisioning a child who might give her parent or teacher little natural opportunity to share in her (the child's) precious goods. If you are the parent or teacher of such a child, work to notice such small moments, thereby creating opportunities to give the child the human affirmation that will promote her growing more connected.

- Keep it simple. You do not need to heap praise on the child. The child would feel overwhelmed and you would soon feel annoyed and depleted. Comments that confirm experience or effort go farther than do those full of excessive flattery. "You worked hard even though you don't like math." "You wore your favorite sweatshirt today." "That chair doesn't feel good, does it?" (Of course, I am assuming that your comments relate to something you observe in the child.) "Thanks for helping me. I appreciate that." You needn't be especially sweet or nice. In fact, many such children often prefer plain and direct to gung-ho and overly enthusiastic.

- Keep it real. Children with Asperger's are often truth seekers. They are not ones for white lies in the name of social grace. "You smell bad," they may declare with utter sincerity and no ill-intent when disliking someone's perfume. Likewise, they often are sensitive detectors of the insincerity of others. They have little use and patience for false flattery, and its use will do little to promote a deeper relationship with them. Saying nice things that you really don't mean will not do much good and may weaken your cause. These children value authenticity, in themselves and in others who wish to be taken seriously.

7

QUIETING SENSORY OVERLOAD

I am kind of weird. I love the smell of skunk and I love the smell of my dog when other people think he stinks. I hate the smell of that grated cheese in the little green shaker, enough so that I would go sit by myself rather than smell that if I had to. I love the smell of garlic, and Italian and Lebanese food, and barbecue and things like burning leaves and logs. I hate the smell of broccoli (though I eat it). I hate the feel of a water drop on my neck when I am outside in the cold, and I hate the itch of dry skin in winter. Bright light literally pains my eyes. I love a head message or getting my head washed before a haircut, but I hate fingers running through my dry hair. A scarf tight around my neck feels good; a tight shirt collar does not. I find TV voices annoying late at night. Fog and dusk and the green of nature relax me. New shoes irritate me; cats make me sneeze. There's no end or apparent rhyme to my sensory likes and dislikes.

My wife is just as weird. The jazz that I adore makes her nervous and gives her a headache. Her eyes cannot have enough sunshine. She loves the smell of any cheese but skunks and grubby dogs offend her. She doesn't like touching certain foods with her hands and she'll use a fork or tongs to pick them up. She doesn't know how I can even stand the foot rubs I adore. She hates the taste of cilantro, parsley, and grape leaves—favorites of mine. Listening to the television at bedtime relaxes her and puts her to sleep. Just like mine, her sensory likes and dislikes go on and on.

Neither of us has, to my knowledge, Asperger's. But our sensory profiles matter to each of us a lot.

Now just imagine that our sensory inclinations were intensified and multiplied. What if I had to eat in a cafeteria that featured grated parmesan on everything and every table? What if I had to endlessly endure bright sunlight and had to work with the sound of a television in the background. As the expression goes, I think I would go nuts.

Imagine being stuck in a small room with a co-worker wearing a perfume that nauseates you, or one that's much too hot or cold. Imagine having to wear clothes made of fabrics that scratch your skin or leave it feeling oily. Assume for a moment that you are an evil doctor in a classic horror flick. Devise a chamber of sensation to torture yourself. I know you can.

Now contemplate what it is like for children with Asperger's. They often experience the regular world as overstimulating and noxious. Much of what you and I take for granted in our environment, sensory stimuli that may not even register with us, can fall on these children like barbed arrows or clouds of suffocating gas. These children ever describe feeling assaulted by the sounds, smells, and so forth of their schools, playgrounds, and homes. Their sensory sensitivities can absolutely plague them day and night, without letup.

Clare Sainsbury's firsthand description of a school environment, as quoted by Attwood (2007, p.272), helps us to see and feel it more vividly:

> The corridors and halls of almost any mainstream school are a constant tumult of noises echoing, fluorescent lights (a particular source of visual and auditory stress for people on the autistic spectrum), bells ringing, people bumping into each other, the smells of cleaning products and so on. For anyone with the sensory hyper-sensitivities and processing problems typical of an autistic spectrum condition, the result is that we often spend most of our day *perilously close to sensory overload.* (Sainsbury 2000, p.101; emphasis added)

I have yet to meet one child with Asperger's who does not suffer sensory sensitivities. Consider Kenneth Hall, who found the chatter of other children as "dynamite going off in [his] ears" (2001, p.39). Kenneth's sensory preferences and dislikes are extraordinarily well defined. He dislikes his hair touching his forehead, cheese grated the wrong size, and mashed potatoes that feel like "paper soaked in water" oozing through "every crevice of [his] mouth" (p.46), whereas he likes the feel of playdough, beeswax, an electric toothbrush, smooth stones, and the soft undersides of certain plant leaves. Though the sensory complaints of the children I've met differ and would compose unique sensory profiles, I know the children would nod in simpatico at Kenneth's well-said complaints.

But what Attwood tells us is yet more remarkable (2007), that some people with Asperger's report their sensory sensitivities as impairing their lives *even more than* their emotional and social problems. If that doesn't say it all, and who of us would have imagined that? Research seems to support our observations. It turns out that, in people who go on to later be diagnosed with Asperger's, sensory sensitivities can be clearly detected when they are babies (Dawson *et al.* 2000).

We all can grasp how concentrating on a task might be difficult when blinded by a tropical sun. That the child can experience the same photophobia perhaps on a gray winter day doesn't make that ordeal any easier to cope with nor does it warrant its being dismissed as unusual so negligible. How intensely can this sensory and hard reality stress and distress a child's life at school and home? Profoundly and pervasively.

Children with Asperger's typically have no choice but to suffer these sensory discomforts in their environments. Like any one of us who, with a horrid headache would give anything for that eardrum shattering leaf blower to just go away, these children would wish for nothing more than their own version of "peace and quiet" whether the stimuli is auditory, visual, olfactory, gustatory (taste) or of touch, mainly via receptors in the skin. That these children try to control their environments speaks, not to their orneriness or wish to disrupt. They are simply trying to free themselves of the sensory oppression that can dog every inch and second of their existence. What experience and reaction could be more human and understandable than that?

How can parents and teachers help the child and her sensory hypersensivity?

- Keep it in mind. Call it an issue of feeling safe or simply freedom from a mere annoyance. Whatever you choose to call it, there's no escaping the fact that any form of sensory overload has to both distract a child's attention and compromise her learning and performance. Helping to "engineer" a sensorily bearable environment for the child will facilitate everything that you later will try to accomplish with the child.

- Ask. Don't be shy to query the child herself about her comfort level. Be specific in your questioning. Is that light too bright? Is it too warm in here? Am I talking too fast, too loud? Some adults find it hard to deal that way with children. They find it makes them feel manipulated or somehow controlled. Remember, the child's wish is not to control you. Her goal is to find comfort in a situation, place, and world in and over which she may feel very little control, and to which, so it feels to her, she is eternally and helplessly subject.

- Observe. Many children with Asperger's are reluctant to make their needs known, even if they're considerable. They may be likely to squint their way through a lesson, rather than ask that the shades be lowered. Watch their behaviors and nonverbal gestures for what they may be expressing and communicating. Autistic mannerisms and tics can exacerbate and intensify under stress, a possible sign that the child is experiencing some stress, perhaps.

- Be responsive. As we will discuss in more detail later, and by virtue of the way they are built neurologically, children with Asperger's tend to know less personal and internal security. They tend to not feel especially comfortable in their own skins, and, according to what I've been told by such children, I am putting it mildly. By responding sensitively to the child's sensory quirks, you will be showing the child that what he experiences matters.

- Teach self-advocacy. By your paying attention to what the child sensorily is feeling, and by responding to that, you demonstrate that you take what the child feels seriously. Your considerate posture for the child's comfort can help teach the child that it is both his privilege and obligation to let others know more openly what he feels and what he needs.

- Use your words. Of course, parents and teachers know how to express themselves in ways that the children do not. Show the child how to express his needs aloud. Perhaps, share your own sensations. "It's getting warm in here. You think we should open the window?" Or, try putting the child's obvious discomfort into words. "No wonder you're sweating. The heat is on much too high." Once you and the child have shared some moments of mutual understanding (around a sensory issue), encourage the child to let you know on his own. "Maybe next time it gets too warm in here, you can just let me know." Rather than suggest that the child is lucky to have your response, let him know that you appreciate his input. "Thanks for letting me know. I think we were all feeling a bit warm."

- Honor the child. Okay, that may sound a bit grandiose and a little, or a lot, too overindulgent. I am not, be clear, saying the child should be flattered, rewarded, or put on a pedestal. That is the last thing the child with Asperger's needs or wants. By honor—a theme that runs throughout his book—I mean, as the dictionary defines it, "regarding with great respect." And what is it that we show such respect to? In this case it is the child's basic sensory experiencing of the world and his (immediate) environment. By doing so, we are respecting the child's neurological reality, his having Asperger's, as it influences his nervous system, in this case his sensory organs (ears, eyes, nose, tongue, and skin) and the way his brain processes their input.

- Don't be arbitrary. There's no need for you to go out of your way to either locate or create sensory disturbances to then react to. Unfortunately, children with Asperger's tend to have an endless supply of such sensitivities and discomforts. The good news is that as you make connection with the child around these stimuli, your need to do so will grow less.

- Problem solve. As you are already anticipating, fixing the environment to fit the child is all well and good, but doesn't he need to learn to live in a world that is full of sensory stimuli and a world that will not be so coddling and responsive? The answer is an unqualified yes! Once the child begins to experience your responsiveness you can help him to learn to cope with what can't or shouldn't be altered. "I know you don't like the smell of the cafeteria. But what you can do, since we can't ask everyone to change what they eat?"

- Stretch the child. Gradually you can nudge the child to experience more of the stimuli that she once was unable to bear a microdecibel of. Perhaps you will start to play the music *you like*, or he'll grow more used to wearing gloves in the cold of winter. As long as the child feels that you truly understand and care, and that you are working with him to better cope with and master the sensory vulnerabilities he knows, he will strive to move ahead with you. No child with Asperger's enjoys these sensory discomforts. He doesn't protest them to vex you, get your attention, or disrupt life at home or in the classroom. His sensitivities represent sensory thorns that he, more than his parent or teachers, wishes he did not have to withstand.

- Strive to bear witness. Sometimes, even though it can't be changed, it feels good just to have someone understand. By sometimes accommodating the child's sensory experiences, by sometimes problem solving the child's coping with them, and by ever striving to notice, acknowledge, and accept them, we tell the child that connecting to what he feels sensorily is worthwhile to us—and himself. And what, more than our genuine and caring response, can (eventually) convince even the child with Asperger's that sharing his experience is a worthwhile thing to do?

- Recognize variability. I've focused on the hypersensitivities of children with Asperger's. In fact, their sensory sensitivities can vary. Some children report hyposensitivity by which, for example, they do not register pain or other sensations until an unusually high threshold is reached. For many more children, their sensory sensitivities fluctuate, depending on the context, degree of comfort, stress, and so on (Bogdashina 2003).

8

QUELLING
ANXIETY

In the late 1980s I had the privilege of meeting a then little known person named Temple Grandin, a woman who we all now recognize as a renowned architect of livestock facilities, and an autistic woman whose books have given the world a profound window into and understanding of the disorder and its experience. Dr. Grandin had come to give the grand rounds lecture at the hospital where I taught. She held us rapt, as she shared her compelling story of a childhood on a farm, her astonishing educational and vocational journey, and her experience with Asperger's.

But, for all of this intrigue and insight, Dr. Grandin took the greatest care to make sure that we heard about the excruciating anxiety that had taken hold of her in her adolescence. She explicitly told us that *we needed to understand that*. Trying to put it in terms we could grasp and relate to, she described it as being like a colossally proportioned case of stage fright that never let up. Dr. Grandin made it eminently clear that this anxiety caused her more suffering and dysfunction *than anything else* she had to confront with Asperger's. And, in fact, when I sat next to her at lunch, I could see that she was far less at ease interpersonally than she'd appeared to be while addressing the packed auditorium earlier that morning.

"He just doesn't know anxiety like the rest of us, does he?" That's what, a few years later, a receptionist in our outpatient clinic had said to me about a boy with Asperger's who was in therapy with me. When I asked what made her say that, she replied that he was a member of her church and that he'd delivered a wonderful sermon to the entire congregation. "He was so calm and collected!" she marveled, adding that she herself could never do that. As one less than perfectly at ease speaking to groups, I could readily identify with what our receptionist had said. But I also knew what I'd seen and felt in my office with this boy.

In my office, I did not see a child who was confident and assured, just the opposite. Timothy's behavior and eventually his talk told me without question that he was beyond extremely nervous with people. He described feeling petrified much of the time when having to interact face to face with people, especially peers. As he put it, despite his perpetual fear of everything, he'd always been able to get up and speak publicly. He didn't know why or how; it just was the way he was. He said that he could feel nervous with even me, and even his parents whom he loved dearly.

Now that I have been working with such children for about 30 years, I have yet to meet a child with Asperger's who does not know a great deal of anxiety. Martin's bodily tension would lead him to fidget constantly and to twist his arms and legs till they almost hurt. He also described interpersonal anxiety that made waiting for his school bus near impossible. He described feeling hot and sweaty much of the time that he had to be near people, especially girls. Wes felt such pervasive anxiety that he, so he said, often could not stop talking lest he lose total control over the anxiety he felt. Timothy, years after we'd first met, articulately described how his high anxiety could literally feel to be tearing him apart, fragmenting him into pieces. Timothy, like many children with Asperger's, did not blush or sweat, but he would grow super rigid and talk more idiosyncratically when having to be with people, especially those he did not know well. A majority of the children with Asperger's that I have known had phobias of doctors, dentists, shots, crowds, dogs, and so forth, phobias that caused them great suffering and could make life difficult for themselves and their parents.

Anxiety was not always seen as a predominant aspect of Asperger's and it is not currently a criterion for diagnosis (APA 2000). In 1981 Lorna Wing cautioned us that Asperger's can look like "diagnosable anxiety." More recently studies show that anxiety symptoms and disorders occur in a majority of children with Asperger's (de Bruin *et al.* 2007; Ghaziuddin, Wiedmer-Mikhail and Ghaziuddin 1998; Volkmar and Klin 2000). Research also supports my own and clinical observations that children with Asperger's tend to have fears that qualify as clinical phobias (Gillis *et al.* 2009; Leyfer *et al.* 2006). To assume that the Asperger child you know may know some anxiety is probably a good hunch. Her anxiety does not have to reach the proportion of a full-blown coexisting anxiety disorder, though it very well can and often does.

This anxiety can present itself in far-ranging and varied ways that can look quite unlike each other, so that parents and professionals are not always sure what they are seeing and not seeing in the child. Some children reveal their anxiety openly and palpably. They fidget and squint and grimace and twitch. Some children with Asperger's can wholly and clearly pronounce their anxiety as did one boy whose puppet, when asked by me what he was scared of, replied, "People, school—maybe I'm afraid of everything." As we went on together, we learned, indeed, that *he was just that.*

Some children know they are big worriers with a capital *W.* "Drive that way," they may tell their parents, striving to direct the show, attempting to control the adults (and kids) in their lives so, as it feels to them, they will be protected from whatever it is that frightens or unsettles them. Much of their obsessions and compulsions may reflect anxieties that they attempt to quell and live with through compulsive behaviors. Wes, a teen who worried excessively about his parents' wellbeing and his own aggressive potential, forever counted his steps, making sure they were of an even number. He likewise tried to control his mother's driving so that she always made an even number of left and right turns. Another boy wrote of worries frequently preventing his sleep, and of a time when he was "petrified for weeks" after swallowing a piece of plastic (Hall 2001, p.53). I have found that many children with Asperger's harbor deep dread that they will lose those they love, particularly the parents they depend upon, pained apprehension that they can not find the words for.

For perhaps a majority of children with Asperger's, their anxiety is not so out in the open. Their fears make themselves known in much more confusing forms. As I wrote elsewhere:

It's easy to identify shaky knees, a quivering voice, sweaty palms, and a fear of snakes. When anxiety shows up in disguise, however—as aggression, arrogance, irritability, impulsivity, anger, [tantrums], or a need to control—it can distract and delay [parents and educators who feel a responsibility] to quickly resolve disruptive or other troublesome behaviors. (Bromfield 2000, p.49)

There is a lot we do not know for sure about the anxiety that children with Asperger's often live with. Is it a byproduct of their neurologically based hardships, especially in the social realm? It is easy to grasp why living in a world that seems to go twice as fast—with its demands, talk, timetables, traffic and social whirl—could make such children anxious. Or is the anxiety they feel more fundamental, arising from the same biological basis that the Asperger's itself comes out of? For our purposes here, it doesn't quite matter. Whether it a distinct co-morbid disorder that exists alongside Asperger's or a mess of symptoms that fall on top of that diagnosis, what we know for certain is that the child suffers and that the burden of that anxiety only makes the child's functioning that much harder and more compromised.

So what are parents and educators to do with the child's anxiety?

- Assume anxiety exists. I know, this sounds contrary to what I have been advising, to study the very child before you. I guess what I really mean is to consider that anxiety exists, even if it is not at first apparent to you. Beware of dismissing anxiety prematurely. Consider it as a hunch as you try to see what makes the child you know tick, especially in ways perhaps that cause him and you difficulty.

- Acknowledge worry. If to worry is human, then children with Asperger's can be supremely human. "That is so worrisome," you can say to a child who has shared a fear. "Of course, that scares you. How could it not?" Having his worry or fear seen and affirmed by a knowing and caring grownup can itself provide a significant sense of comfort and security. That level of acknowledgment can on its own bring a child's fear down to size and make it manageable. When it comes to worry, your sharing will virtually take some of the stress off the child's shoulders, lightening the load of worry he carries.

- Heed the signals. Under stress and duress all of us tend to hunker in and be more like our coping selves. This is equally true for children with Asperger's. When anxious they are prone to do more of whatever they do when stressed. For example, such children may physically tense up, stand or walk with a visible rigidity. Autistic motorisms and tics are likely to re-appear or intensify. The anxious child may talk more and listen less, grow distracted and ornery.

- Look behind and below. A child behaving in an irritable, aggressive, impulsive, and even arrogant way may reflect underlying anxiety. Once you've adequately managed the immediate situation, let yourself observe and wonder whether the child's unspoken anxiety plays a role. If possible, enlist the child in a discussion as to whether that might be. "I know you felt angry. But was the reading assignment upsetting you?" You might notice, for example, that the child gets testier when making transitions or when having to do something new or different.

- Chill. Nothing adds to a child's anxiety more than feeling a parent's or a teacher's anxiety in reaction. The more at ease you can be, the more at ease the child will be. Try not to comment on or critique tics as signs of bodily tension. "Stop that twitching," or even gentler suggestions to that effect, will probably not help. Think of these nervous movements and gestures, not as problems in themselves to be extinguished, but as healthy, comprehensible discharges that will spontaneously go away when they are no long needed, that is, when the child is less stressed and tense.

- Back off. If something you are doing or asking of the child is leading to a sudden or extreme rise in anxiety, slow down and take a breath (for you and the child). Few of us can learn or grow when we are under too much stress. The child who is relatively comfortable and relaxed will learn and perform more effectively. This should not be read as do not push the child or challenge him with work. It means, rather, that excessive stress and strain can prove counterproductive and send your relationship in reverse.

- Mind the gap. Jack Wall, then a director at the TEACCH center in Charlotte, North Carolina, borrowed the term "Mind the gap" from the

London subway system's message for commuters to watch their step when moving between the station platform and the train. Wall suggested that we work to increase the child's awareness of that time and space between an anxiety-provoking event and some behavior, such as a tantrum or angry outburst. "The ultimate goal is to help the child read the signals in his anxiety and expand his 'Decision Zone,' where he can learn to exercise more restraint and [...] come to feel some willful choice in how he responds in the face of a stressor" (Faherty 2000, p.62).

• Explore anxiety. Both parents and teachers can employ the cognitive-behavioral strategies of Tony Attwood's *Exploring Feelings: Cognitive Behavior Therapy to Manage Anxiety program* (2004b). The *Exploring Feelings* program is especially relevant and effective as it goes to the heart of the matter, helping the child to notice, recognize, understand, and process what he feels. Oft times it is vague, amorphous, and overbearing emotion that feels to the child to be a giant ball of anxiety. Coming to learn and know what he feels itself can take much of the heat and pressure out of a child's vague and gloomy sense of anxiety and fear.

• Replay. Karen Levine and Naomi Chedd's *Replays* (2007) offers another doable in-the-moment strategy to help children with Asperger's manage overwhelming and anxiety-provoking situations, events, and demands. Parents and teachers can do this program whenever it's needed, quickly and effectively helping the child to learn from what happened and to do better next time around (that is, the next time he feels such overbearing anxiety). As the child may experience his anxiety much of the time, the parent or teacher's timely intervening can be profoundly reparative and facilitating, and can expedite the child's getting back to the regular business of home or school.

- Condone hang time. Our awareness of the extraordinary stress and anxiety that children with Asperger's can know advises us on one important matter. *Hang time.* It is not coincidence that children with Asperger's crave their unscheduled time as we might oxygen descending from a hike into the Himalayas. Not only might you think twice before ridiculing or dismissing the child's plaint for a break or free time, you might actually beat them to the punch, proactively suggesting that they take a break with a book, or a game or whatever the child finds restorative.

- Seek help and treatment. There is much that a caring parent or teacher can do to help the child's anxiety. The possibilities and potential are near endless and unlimited. However, there will be times when the child's anxiety is causing sufficient suffering or interference as to warrant professional intervention in terms of therapy or medication. Do not hesitate to trust your judgment when you sense such consultation is warranted.

9

FACILITATING COMMUNICATION

Unlike the child with more severe autism, the child with Asperger's acquires language (APA 2000). As we all know, however, that language can differ from that of neurotypical children. Hans Asperger, who wrote about such children more than 65 years ago, described "their difficulty with casual conversation, the odd melody and flow of their speech, and the discrepancy between their immature language abilities and their inclination to big or rarified words and complicated sentences" (as reported in Bromfield 2010a, p.62). Referring to them as "Little Professors," Asperger chronicled examples of what he took to be their capacity for rich and creative use of language, examples including (Asperger 1944/1991, p.71): "I can't do this orally, only headily." "My today sleep was long but thin." "To an art-eye, these pictures might be nice, but I don't like them." "I wouldn't say I'm unreligious, but I just don't have any proof of God."

Around the same time Leo Kanner, a child psychiatrist from Johns Hopkins University, who, like Asperger, was also from Vienna, wrote about such children's language.

Kanner especially noted the impairment, including echolalia (repeating one's own words), misuse and reversal of pronouns, and concrete or literal understanding of words and concepts (1943). About 50 years later Gillberg enhanced our knowledge to include what he called language that was "superficially perfect expressive," "formal and pedantic" with a "flat delivery," and which was typified by "non-verbal communication problems, with limited or clumsy gestures and little or inappropriate facial expression" (1991, p.123).

These formal reports and descriptions will likely lead most any clinicians, parents, or teachers who know a child with Asperger's to shake their head with some recognition or feeling of familiarity. Almost without exception the children with Asperger's that I have met display language that in some way is unusual and that seems distinct for them, that is, unique, not just like every other or any other child with whom they might share the more general diagnosis of Asperger syndrome.

Consider Timothy, a boy with Asperger's whom I treated. Timothy spoke oddly. He made up words and confused pronouns, spoke in a stilted manner with unusual rhythms, and sometimes in a monotone seemingly devoid of emotion, especially when stressed. When Timothy would run to me, excited about a topic, he'd stammer, start and restart sentences, struggling to get his words out. I'd admittedly be tempted to help him get on with it. I could have completed his sentences or filled in the words he desperately sought. But instead I reminded myself that he had *his story* to tell.

"Take your time, Timothy," I'd counsel him. "I can wait to hear what you have to say." Repeatedly, my reassurance would visibly calm Timothy and facilitate his telling me his story the way he needed to. Sometimes, my extrapolating a message from his story also helped him to know that I received what he had to say. "Wow, your story sure shows me just how worried you are about public safety." His replying with a sigh, or a smile, or by telling me that he worried even more about his family's and his own safety, or even my own, let me know that I'd gotten it.

Or think about Frannie, a little girl who, when feeling uncertain, would refer to herself in the third person: "She," the girl would say, "is not so sure about this." I had choices. I could have corrected her grammar and pointed out that she should say, "*I* am not so sure about this." But that might have scared her. Her grammatical misstep, I wondered, may have been unconsciously purposeful, serving to put some distance between her and her feeling. I could have skipped the grammar lesson, but drove the same point home. "Is it you who is so unsure about this?" Or, my pick, I could have replied in the girl's own language. "*She*," I said, "doesn't like feeling so unsure." "No, she does not," Frannie replied sadly. "She doesn't like it much at all." Our subsequent discussion about children and their worries attended more acutely to her feelings, her communication and did more to teach her about the proper use of pronouns than would have any English lesson I might have administered.

Over dozens and dozens of therapy sessions, I and Timothy, Frannie, and all of the other children with Asperger's who've been in therapy with me have created personal languages that we share intimately—made-up words, awkward syntax, bad puns and all. My job was, after all, not to teach them the King's English but to help the children grow (to want to be) more communicative.

That the children grow increasingly desirous of sharing their worlds and experiences with me *through talk and words* is ever a paramount breakthrough that brings enormous satisfaction in itself and which, in turn, makes every other aspect of their social and educational existences easier.

And what about when a young boy runs into my office late, announcing: "My arms are out of breath." Could he have said it any more vividly? And which, in your judgment, of these two responses would have been most helpful? "People and bodies, *not arms*, get out of breath." Or, "Boy, are your arms pooped!" I suspect you know which one I went with.

If I have observed anything with children with Asperger's, it is that the unusual things they say—whether through words they made up, sayings they seemingly confused, mixed-up pronouns—near always say something with a certain meaning. As I said elsewhere, some conventional thinking on autism has tended to mishear and misread the children's words as incomprehensible gibberish, verbal and autistic static to be ignored and extinguished. This thinking might go so far as to rebuke my trying to understand and respond to it, for fear that I will only be rewarding and reinforcing socially inappropriate behavior. As you can tell, my experience compels me to say that I could not disagree more. Deciphering what the child tells me near always leads to some place both fascinating and connected. "At the end of the [therapeutic, home, or school] day, it is the non-Asperger's and utterly human wish to communicate with other humans that most motivates and propels the child with Asperger's" (Bromfield 2010a, p.69).

But how?

- Think about the power of language. Language and words are the currency that make social interaction go round, and that serve as the basis for much about self-understanding and forming a solid and cohesive self and identity. Research tells us that, when it comes to the child's language, apt intervention can not come too early. (And while, I believe, my observations can be of enormous help, they do not replace substantial therapies and interventions that target the child's speech and language.)

- Clarify your priorities. Both parents and educators have a lot they wish to teach and accomplish with the child sitting before them. Recall, though, you seldom can do everything, and for sure, you cannot do everything all at once. While "teaching" proper and effective language are admirable objectives, keep in mind that parents and educators can advance the equally worthy goal of helping the child want to be a better communicator, want to share more verbally with others. Enhancing that basic motivation in the child can powerfully magnify all of the efforts that are made to improve her language.

- Strive to understand. It is easy to dismiss a child's words as nonsense or inadequate. As I've said before, there are some who've suggested that the child's messier verbal expressions be written off as the random static of Asperger neurology. This, I think, is a grave error. Make an effort to meet the child where she is, to ascertain what she is trying to express and convey. Perhaps use her words or phrasing, even if not proper or correct, to show that you get it or are trying to approach the meaning she wants you to get.

- Receive kindly. Some people, we know from our own lives and experiences, are satisfying to talk with. They get it, or at least we know, they try and want to get it. They listen well, patiently, and kindly. Try to be that for the child with Asperger's, though it may be hard. Try not to finish sentences or fill in the blanks, instead letting the child work her way through her own communication. Try to refrain from correcting her grammar or words. Think of how frustrating it is to have someone critiquing your language even as you are trying to express something meaningful. The child with Asperger's feels no less vulnerable, likely more so. Your wanting the child to own her words will help to empower her and build her confidence so that she can capably state her opinions for herself.

- Check in. When you say something to the child, observe and listen that your message has been heard and understood. Do not take it for granted, and do not just let it go as not mattering. If you cannot tell, gently query to see whether what you meant to be heard was heard and understood, as you intended it. Put the responsibility on yourself. Rather than saying to the child with Asperger's, "Tell me what I said," or "Repeat my words" try something more inviting, such as, "I wonder if I made myself clear," or "I don't think I said that too well. Let me try saying it again." Your sincere and caring efforts to be a good communicator, and your willingness to take responsibility for that communication, will enrich the relationship and, for the child, will model a behavior and attitude for her to aspire to.

- Make small talk. I do not mean cocktail hour conversation, of course. In my years of work, I've discovered that no one seems to dislike superficial social conversation more than do children with Asperger's. Using a pun, as might the children themselves, I say small talk as in noticing the little gains that the child makes in communicating with you. Your efforts will bring, not gargantuan miracles as much as steady advancing in the child's wish for, efforts in, and success at communicating in return. Take pride in those inches forward, for, as you know, inches eventually add up to feet and miles.

- Establish the conditions to communicate. Be a good listener. Stop to listen when the child talks, maybe even take a seat if it is a long story. Try not to do five things at once when the child is making a heartfelt effort to express herself. Respect her own nonverbal discomfort while communicating, so as not to stress her when she is trying to talk with you. Work to respond to something in her communication that nurtures even a bit of mutuality and reciprocity. While some children respond positively to enthusiastic and energetic adults, my sense is that a majority of children with Asperger's react most to communication that is plain, direct, understated, well-meaning, and honest.

• Create a language. Allow yourself to enter the child's world and language. While trying to teach them your version of the King's English, take care to heed and respect their version of the language. By allowing yourself to enjoy or admire their language, maybe even their puns or jokes, you will create stepping stones and doorways by which to join with them. If you spend more effort critiquing their language, you will likely miss golden opportunities to share a world and experience with them. There is no better prompt to communicating than sharing a language that is built by both the common word as well as those unusual words, phrases, and meanings that only the child and parent, or child and teacher, know, appreciate, enjoy, and share.

• Promote natural rewards. Behavioral incentives can sometimes motivate children to learn and work at a task, including language. But, while stars or tokens or other prizes may help a child to learn to communicate, there is no more powerful reward for a child's communicating than the feeling of having been heard and responded to. When the child has someone at home or at school whom she likes and trusts to talk with, that is a person and relationship worth understanding and maybe even emulating. When communication grows, it is an endlessly and upwardly spiraling win-win: communication grows clearer; the child shares more; parents and teachers can reach, understand, interact with, and teach the child more dependably and effectively; on and on.

10

TENDING THE INTELLECT

If children with Asperger's are complex, *and they are,* their intellectual and cognitive abilities are often equally so. Their intellects can all at once be a strength and a weakness, be an ally and an obstacle. What do we know about it?

Their intelligence is usually average to above average; that so-called and impressive "splinter skills" can exist even to the level of a savant; interests can be eccentric and all-consuming; executive dysfunction and disorganization are common; verbal skills frequently are much stronger and better developed than are the visuospatial; concentration is a problem; other learning disabilities are common; and, hardly last, social understanding is typically underdeveloped (Baron-Cohen 2008; Thede and Coolidge 2007). In 1944 Hans Asperger worried for these children's futures, and today, research suggests that the prospects for these children are still fraught with danger for underachieving lives full of highly distressing and obstructive symptoms (Saulnier and Klin 2007).

Without question, children with Asperger's often have learning issues that are significant, and which can be significantly supported, compensated for, and even remedied by strong education and intervention. Happily, there is an abundance of able researchers and educators who, even as we speak, are on that case. Fortunately, because of them and their dedicated efforts, children with Asperger's can increasingly avoid the peril of an underachieved life. Much better than that, such children grow to attain substantially and accomplish great things educationally and vocationally. (Make no mistake about it, colleges, graduate schools, and vocations in math, science, computers, engineering, psychology, medicine, business, law, on and on, are replete with highly able and productive men and woman who have Asperger's at a much higher rate than the 1 in 91 found in the general population.)

Recall Timothy. When we began working together he was barely testable. The examiner found him to be intellectually in what's defined as the Borderline to Low Average range (which itself is below the lower end of the Average range). Over the course of therapy, Timothy's performance on periodic psychoeducational testings steadily grew stronger, growing Average and eventually Above Average to Superior. Once a child predicted by mental health authorities to forever live a sheltered and dependent life, he succeeded in school, gained admission to a nationally prominent university where he did well, and has since been employed as a well-paid professional. Once predicted to never ride a bicycle, he not only rode his 10-speed all around Boston (commuting to his high school job as a vendor at Fenway Park) but he learned to drive a car and fly a plane, both at a relatively young age. In short, Timothy grew into an accomplished and independent citizen, a previously unimaginable destiny given what his original IQ testing seemed to indicate.

My many years of working with such children has shown me time and time again that they are capable of learning, growth, and achievement that smash through the glass ceilings that early testings and professionals formerly foresaw. When it comes to children with Asperger's, I've found that IQ scores represent snapshots of functioning that apply to the moment. As children's motivation, attention, engagement, social comfort, and so on advance, so do their ability to take on and succeed in the testing situation. It is worth wondering how high the child's intelligence will go, until proven to settle and stabilize at a specific level.

Even as educational researchers and practitioners further reveal how such children learn (and don't learn), and as they discover more effective methods to target their needs, we have other things to keep our eyes on. Things such as the perfectionism that, unsuspected by parents and teachers, can torment and derail many children with Asperger's. Things such as their obsessions, passions that beside occupying their minds can prove to be the foundation for lifelong and dedicated study, fulfillment, and productivity. When we dismiss or overlook these precious, critical, and relevant things, we put the child's success and development at high risk.

Ellen Winner, a professor at Boston College, has studied and written about gifted children, a good many of whom likely have Asperger's. She makes clear that these children have their own special needs, especially those children more on the extremes—children that she refers to as "severely gifted" (having academic or intellectual strengths many grade levels beyond their peers). The children that Winner studied often possess an extraordinary talent amidst a complex intellectual profile including significant learning disabilities. Winner makes clear her belief that all of us—in the child's home, school, and society—bear a responsibility to notice and nurture exceptional talents (Ellen Winner, in an interview by Howe 1996):

> I know it sounds elitist, but I think it's unfair to treat these children like you treat everybody else, because they're not like everybody else. They know and understand too much too soon and they are feared as strange, oddballs or freaks. But they are America's future leaders and are much less likely to become successful, creative adults if they don't have the right kind of education.

Not all the children she studied had high IQs, as one might expect, nor were they well-versed in all academic and artistic areas, Winner said. However, each of the children displayed an obsession with a particular skill and, whenever possible, looked for or created opportunities to express their specific talent. One with a fervent interest in painting constantly recruited playmates to be his models, for example; another seemed to turn every situation into a mathematical equation, such as calculating distances every time she passed a road sign while on a car trip (Howe 1996).

Even with all of their other difficulties, children with Asperger's need their passions and talents fed and fostered. Without such enrichment and challenge, such children are at great risk to be frustrated underachievers who never find their rightful and productive place in life.

> Maybe, we will do best by following Temple Grandin's advice to not focus too much on the Asperger's diagnosis or label (2008) and instead strive to see the child in his own completeness and reality. Perhaps the child with Asperger's will fare best when we can take his unusual and unique strengths and weaknesses in stride, with an even mix of marvel and responsibility, remediating, supporting compensation, and promoting and enriching, all implemented with our admiration and enthusiasm. (Bromfield 2010a, p.99)

What can parents and teachers do to promote the child's growing intellect?

- Keep IQ scores in perspective. As I said, IQ scores are thought to reveal a child's cognitive abilities. When it comes to children with Asperger's, IQ scores are best thought of as snapshots, cross-sections of a child's intellectual function in that moment of space and time. If you see before you a child who cannot sit still, attend, work, and so forth, you know that will be what the tester sees also, only more so, for the child will also be dealing with the fear and anxiety of being tested and having to sit in a room with someone he likely doesn't know.

- Use your own sensibilities and judgment. If, based on your interactions with the child, you have a sense, or, stronger yet, a conviction that your child or pupil is bright or capable or shows something worthy in some task, trust in it. You can always be shown to have been mistaken or wishful. Hold onto that kernel, core, or island of possibility and nurture

it as you might the last plant on earth. Let yourself
be enthused and hopeful about what you see in the
child, and what you are nurturing.

- Heed the child's pace. As parent or teacher, you may
  feel the pressure to complete tasks or milestones. The
  child may not agree. Rigidly imposing an agenda or
  timetable on such a child can be counterproductive,
  and in the long run lose both of you valuable time,
  relationship, and learning. Nudging and gentle, firm
  shepherding takes more time, granted, but generally
  moves the child faster and farther than do cattle
  prods or proverbial frying pans to the head.

- Be a willing and brave follower. Following the
  child's lead does not mean that she leads you
  blindly by the nose or that she controls you like a
  robotic pet. You heed her needs and lead because
  you understand that Asperger's impacts each child's
  behavioral, cognitive, and emotional ways *uniquely*,
  and that is what you wish to acutely respond to. You
  know that responding that way is nothing at all like
  coddling or being manipulated.

- Use the child's intellect. The child's good thinking
  can be a parent's or teacher's staunchest ally. Let
  the child know what you are up to in plain and
  direct terms. "This exercise," you might say, "can
  help a person understand what another person is
  thinking." Sometimes the child with Asperger's will
  be more willing to engage and cooperate when he
  knows where the demand and the adult behind it
  are coming from. Likewise, a parent, rather than

delivering the customary, "I need you to be less rude (or be nicer) at the family reunion," can try a more intellectual, "Can we have a discussion about the ways of etiquette? They will sound silly and I'd love to hear your opinion about them." Of course, such words and attitude will neither guarantee the child's talking nor his good behavior. It is all about building steps over the long term.

- Befriend the child's interests. We know that children with Asperger's have intense interests that can lead to endless and one-sided monologues and which can drain the child's attention and energy from other types of learning. Try thinking of these interests as passions not obsessions. Instead of seeing them as the enemy or as something to be thwarted, see them as overgrown interests such as we ourselves have. Try to listen and connect with what the child loves about the subject. In my experience, when a child feels that I truly respect his interest, he's more likely to inch toward mine. The more a child feels that you dislike his interest or that it annoys you, the more he'll take it personally and feel a need to withdraw even more into that interest.

- Invite the child's opinions. Exploiting the child's intellect can include asking for his opinions about most anything, from the math problem to world politics to how the classroom is run. You can ask him to think about how his day is spent or what he thinks of the way others treat him. I often find, for instance, that teens with Asperger's enjoy discussing topics of child psychology and development. They may feel clueless and alien to social existence as it happens and yet be thoroughly invested in thinking about social experience as an intellectual enterprise (and, obviously, the latter cannot but help the former).

- Nourish aptitude and talents. With the new economic realities befalling school systems, gifted and talented programs have shrunk and disappeared to become more meager than ever. Seek opportunities and programs for the child to develop their talents and interests. Children whose academic skills warrant it often thrive by attending classes with older children (e.g. a middle schooler taking a math class at the high school). Johns Hopkins University's Center for Talented Youth (CTY) helps to identify and educate gifted children through summer camps and long-distance learning that goes year round. Stanford University has long done the same through its renowned Education Program for Gifted Youth (EPGY) that offers online curricula, especially in mathematics and the sciences, English and history too. Such intellectual experiences can demonstrate to the child that there is a worthwhile and admirable place where he belongs and is valued. Having his talents and strengths acknowledged and responded to may carry the extra benefit of countering the child's frustration and discouragement while he simultaneously works on areas of weakness.

11

CONNECTING TO FEELINGS

Have you ever had the experience of feeling something so intensely, or confusing, or shocking, or mixed-up that you felt utterly overwhelmed by some vague and unsettling stress? Have you ever been so excited, even over something good or wonderful, that your body felt as if it could not contain the feeling? Have you ever been so angry that you couldn't see straight and you felt as if your psyche was crumbling under the pressure? Have you ever felt to be in excruciating conflict, all at once drawn to and repelled by some person, event, or experience? If you have experienced any of these, you at least have an inkling on what the emotional life of a child with Asperger's can feel like.

That children with Asperger's might experience their emotions differently is hardly news. Back in 1944 Hans Asperger described them as "strangely impenetrable and difficult to fathom. Their emotional life remains a closed book" (1991, p.88). Much more recently, Tony Attwood wrote that the child with "Asperger's Syndrome has a clinically significant difficulty with the understanding,

expression, and regulation of emotions" (2007, p.129).
Many such children appear to be "alexithymic," which
means that they lack the words to express what they feel and
thus are unable to express, share or problem solve around
it (Fitzgerald and Molyneux 2004). Although research
debates whether these differences reside in fundamental
neurophysiology or at higher brain processing (Ben
Shalom *et al.* 2006; Critchley *et al.* 2000; Minio-Paluello
et al. 2009; Willemsen-Swinkels *et al.* 2000), it agrees with
what clinicians, parents, and educators know firsthand: for
children with Asperger's, emotional experience is a stress
and a challenge.

I often find, in the children with Asperger's who I
treat, that they react to any and all feelings with some
individually characteristic and predictable behaviors. For
example, one boy I recently saw in therapy reacted to
every feeling with a disturbing stew of irritability, anger,
excitement, and hyperactivity. The precise nature of the
precipitating event or circumstance seemed not to matter.
His body tensed and charged but he was unsure what it
was that he felt beneath the arousal. Getting in trouble at
school drove him to this hyperstate as did the good feeling
of a school day well done. Having his parents tell him
that he would be punished or that he'd lost some privilege
led to the same, as did their telling him that he would be
earning something special. It was as if his body had one
main circuit that lit up the same with any form of feeling,
and which when turned on overrode the body's capacity
to handle the charge. And so, under the sway of most any
feeling, whether positive or negative, the boy—meaning
his body and nervous system—needed to discharge in
a form that usually involved verbal anger, tantrums, and

aggressive behaviors. Our productive therapeutic work focused on slow, steady, belabored, and careful affirmation, acceptance, and problem solving around the precipitating circumstances and emotion.

But these findings in no way prove that children with Asperger's lack an emotional life, or that they don't feel the same feelings as you, I, or their neurotypical peers. The preconceived notion that, because they are not effusively expressive, children with Asperger's don't feel as much may be a misguided one. While it is true that they may take a longer time to process their feelings, and may express them less articulately, research shows that children with Asperger's can, for instance, feel and understand jealousy, pride, embarrassment, and guilt—emotions that have social relevance and seem to be complex (Bauminger 2004; Bauminger, Chomsky-Smolkin *et al.* 2008). Some studies suggest that children with Asperger's feel very intensely, perhaps too much so. I personally have known many boys with Asperger's who feel things and life deeply. Sitting in their presence, their emotional reserve felt nothing like impassive or shallow; it felt intense and pained. Other studies have documented that even rather young children with Asperger's experience differentiated feelings, including shame. Shame, by the way, has appeared to me to be a primary emotion often felt by the child with Asperger's, a humiliating self-dislike that can descend upon the child like a heavy black curtain. Overwhelming feelings of shame are often the main obstacle to a child's being able to own and show remorse for a misbehaving deed. Admitting what one did and amending for it is just too painful.

Last, I must make bold mention of depression. Like anxiety, clinical depression and milder depressive symptoms are exceedingly common, especially in the adolescent with Asperger's. Why? Probably some admixture of the syndrome itself, the hardships it creates, the misunderstanding, the social isolation, the bullying, and so forth. Ironically, it seems that sometimes the brighter and more aware the teenager with Asperger's, the more pronounced is the susceptibility to depression. Whatever the causes of that depression, it must be taken as seriously as it should be taken in any child or teenager. Depression, and its symptoms, should never be written off as just the side effects of having Asperger's or as something that the child will grow out of. Children with Asperger's can fall into deep black depressions just as they can commit suicide.

Having Asperger's grants no immunity when it comes to depression. On the contrary, the stress of having Asperger's and the possible lack of a social network can make the child, and especially the teenager with Asperger's, that much less fit to cope with depression, whether it comes from the Asperger's itself or in combination with the trials of adolescence. Do not hesitate to refer the depressed child with Asperger's for therapy or to be evaluated for the suitability of antidepressants.

This chapter is just the tip of the iceberg, a virtual distilling of the complicated and messy landscape known as the child's emotional life. Suffice it to say that both parents and teachers sit in a perfect seat from which to notice and respond to the child's feelings, including her difficulties thereabout. Keep in mind that whatever methods and goals you pursue on the way to raising the child's Emotional Intelligence (EI), what matters most is what the child is feeling in that very moment. That immediate "space," between parent and child, or teacher and child, is the heart of it all; it's where the action and potential for remedy reside.

Here are some strategies to help your child or student better recognize and manage her emotions:

- Be emotionally available. Try to be open to the child's emotional state. This can be hard with a child who herself may be so clueless who, as the cliché goes, might well be the last one to know what is emotionally going on inside her. Let yourself be interested in what the child might be feeling.

- Affirm what the child feels. How does a child grow to better see and identify what she feels? By feeling it, and by having someone trustworthy travel alongside affirming and accepting what she is experiencing. At first it might be as generic as: "Boy, you are so excited your body doesn't know what to do." Gradually, you might connect the feeling to an event. "I corrected you and now you are running around wild." The child's gestures, actions, and maybe words will let you know whether your intuition is right or amiss. Eventually, as an example, you might be able to tie together for the child that she ran wild because your criticism made her feel bad.

- Take the child's feelings seriously. When you dismiss what a child feels, you unavoidably dismiss the child herself. That the child is tentative with and fearful of her own feelings can give you a big heads-up. Big and moderate feelings are just too much for her to hold onto and deal with. And so, you start with small feelings, over small occurrences, or that come in small doses to small degrees. "That lunch disappointed you." "You don't like this word problem, do you?" Receiving such understanding helps the child to tolerate her own unsettling emotions such that she starts to grow in her capacity to function alongside them.

- Label feelings. Encourage the child to try to name what it is that she is feeling. Simply referring to her *anger, jealousy, resentment, sadness,* and so on can start to give her a shorthand that allows her to know what she feels a bit better, and to communicate that in ways that are easy, quick, and relatively effective. Though she still might be unable to fill you, and herself, in on why she is so distressed, she might be able to at least convey feeling defeated or self-hating.

- Encourage the child to use words. Related to her learning to name her feelings, she is using her words to express what she feels more fully and in detail. Children with Asperger's often have strong vocabularies and impressive verbal skills. Gently urge the child to work at applying those formidable resources to the expression of what she feels. Strive to be patient, curious, and accepting as she awkwardly or with stammers attempts to communicate her feelings and the situations that underlie them.

- Honor strongly felt and expressed feelings. When it comes to self-expression, I've found that children with Asperger's can be a bit like rusty faucets that, once rattled, just burst open with unexpected force.

While teachers may not be able to accept cursing or other strong words—and many parents feel the same way—beware of critiquing the child when she does come to express herself full force or directly. Many adults will not tolerate children saying things like "Fuck off!" or "I hate you." If you must curtail such expressions, do not negate the feeling. Try to show some acknowledgment for the feeling that is being let out. "I know I've angered you, but I do not wish to be spoken to like that." "Please find some other words to tell me how much I'm frustrating you" or, perhaps, "please write down all that you want me to hear and know." Keep in mind that strong words serve as way stations as the child matures from pure (impulsive) behavior toward self-control.

- Monitor your own emotions. Children with Asperger's may look blind to other's feelings but they actually can be very attuned and reactive to what those around them are feeling, especially the adults whom they dearly depend on and interact with. It is good for the child to experience, learn to recognize, and deal with your own emotional responses to them. Your excessive or perennial frustration or anger, however, can overwhelm them, and lead to their withdrawing from you. Robert Hughes, in writing about his own experience parenting a child with Asperger's, described it as: "Firm, Friendly, Not Freaked Out" (2003, p.51).

- Work the child. Just as with anxiety, take advantage of solid books that offer both parents and teachers programs to continually work with the child at home or school on learning to better recognize, process, and manage her emotions. Attwood's *Exploring Feelings* series applies cognitive-behavioral principles to both anger and anxiety (2004a, 2004b). Levine and Chedd's *Replays* (2007) offers a strategy by which either parent or teacher can help a child "dissect" a behavioral meltdown, helping her to identify the emotional precipitant and problem solving better ways to cope with such stress and feelings in the future.

• Do not turn away from depression. I am repeating myself here for it is such a critical point. Whether by way of its basic neurology or as a result of its hardship and realities, children with Asperger's often know depression, especially adolescents. With the irony that typifies so much of human existence, so much of what Asperger brings—social disconnection and isolation, emotional confusion, learning problems, and so on—makes the child with Asperger's only that much more vulnerable. Know too that, while depression in the adolescent can be visible, depression in younger children can first and predominantly manifest itself as irritability, frustration, and aggression. Reach out, and seek professional help—whether for therapy or medication.

• Connect. Keep in mind, at the very top of your list, in capital and bold letters, that *every molecule of connection you forge with the child helps to protect her from the toxicity of isolation, self-hatred, despair, and depression.*

12

PROMOTING FRIENDSHIP

If there is anything a parent or teacher of a child with Asperger's knows, it's the social difficulties—the awkwardness, the rejection, the bullying, and the isolation. It's the loneliness.

While the social deficits of Asperger's adversely affect most every aspect of the child's life, its most distressing impact is the way it obstructs the making and keeping of friendships. The stress and failure of their social experience can make the child with Asperger's depressed (Barnhill 2001) and aggressive (Simpson and Myles 1998), and can leave the child ever exhausted, physically and mentally (Attwood 2007, p.17). Asperger's might be at the higher end of the spectrum, and yet it remains "a highly socially disabling condition" (Tantam 1991, p.178). Hans Asperger himself took the "limitation of their social relationships" to be the "fundamental disorder of autism" (1944/ 1991, p.77).

Anyone who spends much time with a child with Asperger's soon learns that he indeed has a need and want for social connection, however much that need and want may appear different from our own or those of neurotypical children. The yearning is palpable, even as we observe and personally experience the factors that get in the way of a relationship: the single-minded interests, self-absorbed talk, relative lack of empathy, off-putting and asynchronous body posturing and gestures, and so forth. That the child with Asperger's may not be naturally outfitted to get the friends he wants doesn't undo or minimize his wish that he might.

Consider for a minute what friends can do for one another. They offer partners in fun and activities. Friends offer companionship that can help to assuage feelings of inadequacy. The support of friends can help keep a child afloat when life and its stresses grow rough. Friends teach a child about relationships, sharing, generosity, and resolving conflict. Friends give a child meaningful others to care about, compare oneself to, compete with, and be inspired by. The child with Asperger's wish for friends is anything but a baroque worry. Not having friends is a true loss in every conceivable way, and it reminds us of the way that the child with Asperger's gets hit two times, first by his social deficit and, second, by the loss of friendship along with its life lessons and sustenance.

But, before you rush out to try to help your child or pupil make friends, there's more to tell. When it comes to children's friendships, we need to think small and careful. Sound research shows that it is not about being popular and the number of friends. Becoming a social butterfly is not the goal—as if it ever could happen. Can you guess what kind of friendship endows a child with the most positive influence and surest protection against depression, poor self-esteem, and bullying? You are right. One best friend is all it takes. One good chum. That chum, in turn, does not have to have a high social valence, meaning that friend does not need to himself or herself be popular, cool, or even another person's best friend. Merely having your own best friend can do wonders for the child. It can do more for the child with Asperger's.

Children with Asperger's can learn to get along better with other children by being with them, especially under the skilled and gentle eye of an adult who can facilitate the child's social learning and change. Some schools have sensitive psychologists, counselors, social workers, and other specialists who meet with such children in group settings. Some programs teach children *social pragmatics*, skills and strategies for interacting with other children. The research further tells us that children with Asperger's benefit from socializing with nonautistic as well other children who have vulnerabilities similar to their own. For the child with substantial social anxiety, evaluation for medication can also be beneficial.

It was once questioned whether the child with Asperger's even had interest in friends. Newer research shows that children with Asperger's have much greater social interest than was previously believed. They also have more understanding about friendship and relationships, even if that understanding is less and limited compared to what his peers possess (Carrington, Templeton and Papincazak 2003). Studies that observe real children in real groups have documented that children with Asperger's take more action than thought when it comes to making friends. But they are not as deft at it and they are not as adept at keeping the relationship moving and growing (Bauminger, Shulman and Agam 2003). Of course, we also have to reckon with the reality that the child's appeals for friendship, even when reasonable, may not be welcomed and returned as parent, teachers, and the child himself might wish for.

There are other things we are wise to remember when pondering and "working" on the child and his social skills. Being alone is not the enemy to be avoided. The individual need for social connection varies, each and every one of ours. The child is neither bad nor defective for wanting more alone time than you might judge is good for him. As I said before, private hang time can be a cherished commodity for the child with Asperger's, especially after a trying and hard day at school.

There are, as an adult and nonautistic client once conceptualized to me, two kinds of people. The first kind are social. They renew their battery, so to speak, by feeding off the energy of others. A weekend without parties depresses and tires them. The second kind of people are just the opposite. They like being with people, to a degree. But being with people drains their battery. These people replenish themselves by reading, staying home, taking a solitary walk. A majority of children with Asperger's, I think it's fair to say, tend to be more like the second kind of people. That is okay for that is who they are; *it has to be okay.*

Many children with Asperger's are rather contented and even happy when alone. That does not make them hermits. It makes them people who often prefer their own company. Our goal—as parent, teacher, or therapist—is not to make the child popular or social beyond his own interests. It is primarily to help enable him to be more socially connected with the people that he wishes to be closer to, to help him have the skills, confidence, and trust to make happen the relationships and human contact he himself longs for or imagines as part of a fulfilling life.

This last piece of advice reminds us too of a basic truth that runs throughout this book. The child with Asperger's has a true self that he wishes to grow into and develop ever more coherently and cohesively. The relatively new field of girl and women's psychology taught the dangers of a society that raised girls to hide or sacrifice their true beings, instead cultivating false selves that took them to emptier, less meaningful, perilous, and unhealthy places. Published authors with Asperger's have warned us of the high costs of living a life that is false and a façade. Many people with Asperger's have gone through life pretending to be what they were not. This is always a bad choice. While having friends is a good thing, abandoning one's own authentic self is never a worthwhile price to pay. The child with Asperger's needs and deserves friends. He doesn't need or deserve friends who are not interested in connecting with the person he truly is.

What can parents and teachers do to help the child with Asperger's find friendship?

- Assume the child cares about friendship. Try assuming that the child wants to be socially connected to others, even if it is not otherwise apparent. My 30 years of working with these children has shown me that they have wishes for friendship that neither their words nor behaviors give any indication of.

- Accept the child as she (socially) is. Even as you may work to teach the child new ways of being social, remain compassionate for her being the way she is, which includes for her behaving in ways that, to onlookers' eyes, seems to be anything but socially inviting. Why can't she just do things a bit differently so as to be more socially approachable, you might wonder to yourself, frustrated that you cannot get the child you love or care for companionship and friendships? Why indeed? If she didn't have to be that way, she probably wouldn't have Asperger's.

- Respect the child's social ambition (or lack thereof). If the child says she doesn't like Brandi—and you have no reason to doubt her—then you might refrain from pushing her to be Brandi's friend. Would you want someone like me telling you who to socialize with? Likewise, parents and teachers especially need to take care not to push the child into situations that she cannot or doesn't wish to deal with, at least not yet.

- Go slowly. Growing socially can be a labored and snail-paced process. When it goes right, it goes slowly and surely. And the child leads the way. If you wish to try play dates, for example, keep them short and be ready to bail them out quickly if they start to deteriorate. Bad social experiences do nothing to help the child grow, feel better about herself, or make headway with her peers. There may be no such thing as bad advertisement, but there certainly is a thing like bad social experiences that would have been better had they never happened, that send the child and her social growth backward.

- Reframe the child's social avoidance and discomfort. In trying to explain the profound experience of his son's relationship with a therapist, Robert Hughes wrote, "One of Maureen's gifts was her sense that Walker's problem was like ordinary 'shyness' taken to the hundredth power" (2003, p.142). This conception of a nuclear-proportioned case of shyness, for example, is a pretty good guide by which to interact with such a child, probably a better guide than might be a sterile, neurologically loaded definition. After all, most of us can figure out what might work with an exquisitely shy child. Most of us will know it requires things such as going slowly, patiently, carefully, and so on.

• Think activity. Research shows that "activities with friends are an important part of the daily lives of children" (Mathur and Berndt 2006). This same research says that the type of the activity is irrelevant, whether clubs, athletics, or—dare I say—just listening to music, watching movies, or playing videogames. The child's following her own passions may sometimes be the shortest route to sharing an activity with peers, especially for tweens and adolescents.

• Foster equal opportunity. Should the children with Asperger's be steered to make friends with other children with Asperger's, with children who have other types of learning problems, or with generally neurotypical peers? The research suggests that you needn't lose sleep over the question for children with Asperger's profit from interacting with children of all sorts, with and without similar difficulties (Bauminger, Solomon et al. 2008). What matters is whether the child feels a connection, a click of friendship with that other child.

- Keep it in check. Both parent and teacher want the best social experiences for the child. Friendship and enhanced social interaction are worthy and wonderful goals. But this kind of growth comes slowly, even when steady and encouraging. Beware of getting overly enthused or wanting to move it along faster than the child wants or can handle. Respect the child's pace, and you will protect against the child feeling overly pushed, such that her only option is to retreat.

- Be a good chum. The psychiatrist Harry Sullivan wrote:

  > If you look very closely at one of your children when he finally finds a chum, you will discover something very different in the relationship— mainly that your child begins to develop a real sensitivity to what matters to another person. And this is not in the sense of "what should I do to get what I want," but instead "what should I do to contribute to the happiness and to support the prestige and feelings of worth-whileness of my chum?" (1953, pp.245–6)

  By being a good friend to the child yourself— honoring who he is—you will offer a caring and responsive relationship that shows and teaches the child what a relationship between friends can be.[1]

---

1 I've purposely left out the subject of bullies and mean girls here, though I will touch on them in a later chapter on gender. There are many good books available that address this matter in detail and that offer constructive advice, including: Attwood's chapter "Teasing and Bullying" (2007, pp.85–111); Iland's chapter "Girl to Girl" (2006, pp.33–63); and Dubin and Carley's book *Asperger's and Bullying* (2007).

13

GIVING AND NURTURING EMPATHY

Empathy.

As you have long caught onto, the concept of empathy beats at the heart of this book. It is the essence of your relating to the child with Asperger's, the trustworthy guide to all of your responding, interacting, and intervening. Whether you are dealing with the child's feelings, depression, anxiety, intellect, sensory sensitivities or social experience, empathy is all at once the goal, the medium, and the message. But for all of the way in which empathy has been implied and spoken of directly so far, I need to make it clearer. If I had to rely on just one chapter from this book to convey my thinking, it would be this chapter on the offering of empathy.

That children with Asperger's lack empathy is a familiar refrain, almost a defining hallmark held up by much of the professional community in autism. If you go through the indices of the most popular books on the subject you will find rare entries for the word "empathy," and most of them direct readers to a briefly stated headline that state in no uncertain terms that children with Asperger's don't have any of it. The discovery and proof that autism is a disorder of neurodevelopment (Happé and Frith 1996) was accompanied by research showing such children lack what is called a "Theory of Mind," meaning the ability to recognize, grasp, and make sense of another person's thinking and feeling (Baron-Cohen 1989; Frith 2001; Frith, Happé and Siddons 1994). When it came to empathy, parents, teachers, therapists, and the children themselves were painted a picture that was neither pretty nor encouraging.

I am not here to say that this research is faulty or mistaken. It is not. Nor are the researchers and thinkers behind such work who represent the yeomen and "yeowomen" who've dedicated their lives, careers, and brilliance to unraveling the mysteries of the autistic brain and its cognition. What I am here to say—no, I mean, here to yell from the rooftops!—is that the reality is more complicated and hopeful. My decades of working with such children have shown me that such children do have empathy, empathy that can be nurtured and grown.

What though, we must first ask, is *empathy*? It is not the same as sympathy or pity, though both involve compassion and sad feeling for another person's misfortune. We can hold sympathy or pity or feel bad for someone for whom we have little or no empathy. Although it involves taking another person's perspective, empathy implies something deeper and more connected. Baron-Cohen (2003) sees it as having two parts: a cognitive understanding of what the other person is going through, and two, an emotional reaction that resonates with that person's dilemma.

Lampert beautifully defines it as "what happens to us when we leave our own bodies [...] and find ourselves either momentarily or for a longer period of time in the mind of the other. We observe reality through *her* eyes, feel *her* emotions, share in *her* pain" (2005, p.157; emphasis added). Though empathy has long been an object of formal study, we probably all know what we mean when we say we're in tune with another person's experience, when we feel for her, when we're on the same wavelength, or when we walk in her shoes. And, while we may ourselves lack the words to explain or describe empathy as a concept and phenomenon, we sure know when we get it—and, more so, when we don't.

My clinical experience has convinced me without any doubt that children with Asperger's have empathy, of all sorts. Many of the adolescents I've seen with Asperger's have uncanny intellectual awareness of what another's circumstance might be like. I've seen several children with Asperger's, both young and old, who possess an acute radar to detect the moods of others. A piece of recent research supports what I've seen, finding that children with Asperger's can resonate with [another] person's emotional experience as well as neurotypical children (Rogers *et al.* 2007). Also in my clinical experience, I've observed that children with Asperger's seem to be most empathically sensitive with those they are closest to, with whom they experience a relationship. Most critical as we try to imagine what the impact of our empathic responses might be to the children, they, I've found, are especially sensitive to others' anger toward, frustration with, disappointment in, and rejection of them, even when unspoken. Many such children seem to have radar that accurately detects such negativity (and positivity, too). In fact, one recent study in neuroscience suggests that some children with Asperger's may experience fear and withdraw as a result of their being overly attuned to and overwhelmed by others' emotional states. This so-called "Intense World" theory of autism hypothesizes that children with autism may suffer from too much "neuronal information processing" and not too little (Markram, Rinaldi and Markram 2007).

And flipping empathy on its head, we need to confront the sad truth that the child with Asperger's gets much less empathy than do neurotypical peers and adults. It's not because, I stress, her parents don't love her as much or her teachers don't care enough. They likely do. It is mostly because such children can be hard for others to relate to, to understand, to feel the world and her Asperger experience through her eyes, ears, and brain. As I wrote elsewhere: "This is forever her problem. *But it should be ours*" (Bromfield 2010a, p.165).

"Not one of us gets the understanding we want, and few get as much as we need. Leroy got less, much less." That is how I once began a case history about a boy with Asperger's (Bromfield 2010b, p.59). Though our prolonged work together would take a book in itself, that first line kind of says it all. What did Leroy and I accomplish together? *We created a place and relationship in which profound and mutual understanding took place.* Period. I think if we'd been able to attain nothing else, that alone would have amounted to something huge, meaningful, and therapeutically successful. That the child with Asperger's hungers for understanding—albeit in a form and manner to their liking and tolerance—has been taught to me over and over as a basic truth.

In an episode from the original *Star Trek*, Captain Kirk and his crew encounter a mute woman who they name Gem. When Kirk cuts his forehead, an identical and bleeding wound appears on Gem's forehead. Gem's wound soon heals, and when Kirk touches his own forehead, he finds that his wound has healed and disappeared. Gem, they soon learn, is an *Empath*, a creature so exquisitely attuned to others, she can sense and alleviate their pain almost before they themselves feel it. Though we'd all like to have a friend like Gem, she exists only in science fiction.

As a therapist and somewhat empathic person, I often say and do the wrong thing. Well, *wrong* is not what I mean, for it suggests an error that should have been avoided. I mean that sometimes I ask or say things that make the child or adult sitting across from me feel bad, or hurt, or somehow offended. I guess, if I did that frequently enough, it might make me unsuited to be a therapist. But I can promise you that all therapists have their fair share of such moments. While, like parents and teachers, we might aspire to be thoroughly empathic, we inevitably fall short of that ideal. Then again, would being perfectly empathic be a good thing, even if we could?

Ponder this situation that happened at a family company picnic that a child and his mother went to. The boy, in a characteristic moment of sincerity, had told his mother's boss that he's a "man who treats his mother poorly." Terribly embarrassed in front of her employer, the mother rebuked her son sternly for making stuff up. Understandably shaken, she took him aside and yelled at him to "grow up" and to "learn to keep his mouth shut."

The boy kept to himself for the rest of the picnic. Once in the car on the way home, he couldn't help but defend himself. "But you always say those things about him." His mother felt terrible. She immediately realized that she'd humiliated her son in public, and worse, that while unfairly accusing her son of "making things up," she'd been the one not telling the truth. How did this mother repair the damage done?

She simply admitted what happened. She acknowledged that her son always heard her complaining and that he'd tried to stick up for her against the boss whom she feared. "You were not the liar, I was," she said. "What I did was cowardly but what you did was brave." Once the boy felt understood, that his perspective was empathized with, he and his mother were able to have a constructive first step for a long conversation concerning private and public communication.

What the child with Asperger's needs from other people is for them to be as human with him as they are with all children. To be human, of course, is to be imperfect in all ways, including empathically. As I'll soon describe, by experiencing others in her life admit their empathic failures *empathically* in itself conveys understanding and empathy that nurtures the child's own kernel of empathic potential. While I grasp the inordinate value of cognitive and behavioral programs to train social skills, in my experience it is the human relationship *in vivo* that wields the greatest powers with all children, including those with Asperger's. Ultimately, or at least to a profound degree, it is receiving empathy that begets growing one's own empathy (for others).

How can we give and nurture empathy?

- Assess your relationship for empathy. Try your best to answer this question candidly to yourself: To this day, how empathic have you been to the child or student with Asperger's that you know? This is not an exercise in guilt or self-whipping. Nor should you feel bad or apologize or suddenly say a million and one empathic things, as if one could ever do that. This observational meditation is simply to help you to see what the reality of your relationship with the child has been.

- Seek to know the child's inner reality as well as the outer. I once asked a professor at a university library where fiction was kept. He replied, "Wouldn't you rather read about truth and reality?" Any good reader of good literature knows that it reveals the human condition in great candor and Truth. Likewise, what the child feels, thinks, dreams, and so on, has an equal veracity and realness. What goes in the inside is as real as what goes on in the outside world.

- Learn to reflect. The mechanics of giving empathy are simple. Once you come to see or understand what the child experiences, you show that you get it. Repeating what the child says in your own words— or his words—can feel odd at first. But it soon grows natural, and can work small miracles. The child with disgust spits out spinach. "I won't eat this." And the parent merely replies, "You don't like spinach." Read Hiam Ginott's small, classic *Between Parent and Child* (2003, the umpteenth reprint of the original 1955 work), which wonderfully shows how parents can listen and reply more responsively.

- Observe and reflect first. Ginott wrote his book hoping to help parents better understand and manage their child's behavior. He knew the magical power that good and responsive talk can have on a child. At its best, such mutual understanding can often wholly eliminate the child's need to assert his feeling through oppositional actions or other misbehaviors. For example, a child wears his hooded parka drawn tight during his math class. The teacher can confront this, and demand that the coat come off. A savvier teacher might try saying, "You must be cold, wearing that parka inside." Such a neutral, accepting remark will likely do more than will any testier demand.

- Repair empathic failures. As I said earlier, none of us is perfect, empathically or otherwise. The goal is not to strive to be ever empathic. But we do need to admit when we miss the mark. Let's say the child shows you a drawing that, however odd and messy, she is proud of. You say, "God, that's a mess. Why is the tree all black and gross?" Likely empathic failure, we agree? How can you recover after committing empathic failures? Admit it, to yourself and the child. "You wanted me to see your drawing, and I asked a dumb question." The child does not need a profuse apology or compensatory flattery. All she needs is acknowledgment that you did not respond as she would have wanted you to, and as she had appealed to you to do (by showing you her creation in the first place).

- Do not punish or reject the child for your empathic failing. Nothing feels worse than to have the person who hurt us, then turn around and give us further grief or punish or reject us for our reasonable reaction. What can we say when we mess up empathically? "You're right. I was not listening well." "I missed the point." "I get why you are upset with me." Remember, empathic failures themselves are part of life, especially the life of a child with Asperger's. Usually, the world-at-large does not bother to notice and admit its empathic shortcomings to the child. That you do will be welcomed generously inside the child, even if she doesn't show it to you. Remember, too, that repairing empathic failures is a learning experience for both you and the child, one that only helps to grow trust and connection.

- Strive for sincerity. Children with Asperger's are particularly sensitive to phoniness and dishonesty. Empathy that is faked, that is just gone through the motions to somehow get it over with or to manipulate the child's behaviour, will not work, and will paradoxically undermine your relationship. If you cannot be sincere with the child, try to find out why you cannot.

- Beware of frustration and anger leading the way. Anger and frustration can unconsciously block your feelings of empathy and understanding for the child. When you find yourself feeling negatively toward the child or your work and efforts with her, take action to understand why and try to let it go enough to be there for the child. Use trusted colleagues, friends, families, or professionals to find support, relief, and insight into your feelings and difficulties with the child.

- Don't forget to smell the garbage. It is pretty easy to empathize with hearts and flowers. "You like me so much. I can see that." It is much harder to empathize with feelings such as: "You really hate this class." "You really don't like me." "You wish you still had Mrs. Anderson instead of me." On and on. Remember, the child with Asperger's goes through life so alone with what she feels and with what no one else seems to be able to comprehend and understand. To have that stuff seen, affirmed, and empathized with cannot help but feel to be a supremely loving moment of warmth, closeness, and gratitude for such a child.

- Forgive yourself. The goal is not to be the perfect empathizer but to notice when you have missed the mark. Give the child and yourself the opportunity to repair your relationship. The child seeks and needs no more than that.

- Don't expect a thank you note. When the child feels your empathy, she will probably not thank you or light up or say anything dramatic to let you know. But, if you're watching, listening, and feeling, it will be clear to you that your empathy was received and that it touched the child. You might see a child who looks just a molecule lighter and calmer, or who is a little less oppositional, or whose tic eases up. Empathy can be conveyed by all sorts of words, gestures, actions, and silences. Empathy can be expressed poignantly in a smile, a handing of a pencil, or a simply letting the child be.

14

FEEDING
CREATIVITY

Conventional wisdom and an abundance of research has said that children with Asperger's cannot do play therapy because, so went the logic, they lack the capacities to play, pretend, and imagine (Baron-Cohen 1987; Harris and Leevers 2000; Hobson, Lee and Hobson 2009; Lord *et al.* 2000; Ungerer and Sigman 1981; Wulff 1985). Not so long ago, the "National Autistic Society itself [once] cite[d] a 'lack of creative pretend play' as one of the features characteristic of the syndrome" (Jarrold, Boucher and Smith 1993, p.281; it no longer does). The facts state *what is*, and we have no good reason not to believe that whatever relative lack exists is based in neurology. This reality, however, does not dampen what children with Asperger's have continually shown me about their ability to play and create, albeit *in their own way*.

Think back to Timothy, a boy I treated for many years. He spent countless hours drawing maps of two subway lines, maps that he transformed into three-dimensional maps that included paper models of actual subway stations, where animal puppets and play figures waited anxiously for the next train. Was it pretend enough that Timothy had the two of us stand in the corner of the office, holding our hands up as if grabbing the ceiling handles, wobbling as if balancing ourselves on the moving train? (Timothy, after all, knew perfectly well that my office was not the real subway train.) Was it creative enough that he, on his own at home between sessions, built props that adorned his play, props such as the conductor's dashboard of the train or token and ticket transfers? What if I tell you that he evolved this play over many months to deal with the dismantling of one subway line and its replacement with another? What if I add that this play, and dynamic, in turn, reflected his pained grieving for the loss of a beloved therapist and his having to reconnect with another, mainly myself?

Or, consider the girl who, detesting herself for what she called her "weirdness"—meaning her Asperger-related in-your-face awkwardness with other children—created a stunning play scene in which a dinosaur was killed by an angry crowd who thought the beast "too ugly and too awful" to share the planet with. With tears and sadness, that girl cleaned up after her play, assuring me that I shouldn't feel bad for the dinosaur because it deserved to die. Or, how about the young boy who built us homes out of blocks, and then decorated them. Some of the furnishing came at face value, such as a pillow and shawl to be a blanket. He used other things, too, toys and building structures, to represent a television, clock, and other bedroom items. Whether pretending to march in a holiday parade, go to a much feared doctor's visit, or cook a feast in a play kitchen, I've often discovered that children with Asperger's play up a storm. Indeed, speaking of storms, one child pretended to be caught in a whirling tornado, while another child asked that I get out of the only imagined "rain" by joining her under the umbrella that she'd built out of Tinker Toy sticks.

The play and creativity of children with Asperger's do not have to resemble our preconceived notions of what (neurotypical) play and creativity should look like, as if there is a standard. Creative play can be assembling your playing cards into new and interesting decks. Creative play can involve lining up toy trucks to form letters or to give the overhead impression of an urban traffic jam. I have witnessed dozens of children, with and without Asperger's, using my magnetic building set to assemble marvelously complex, dazzling, and unexpected structures that they, in turn, subject to experimentation and proudly display.

Children with Asperger's have drawn for me, made origami animals and shapes, sculpted, woven lanyard jewelry, and reorganized my office in new and interesting ways. They've used the tall conga drum to make rhythms and music, sometimes incorporating other items to be a one-man band. Children with Asperger's often take the standard children's board games I have and remake them with new layouts and rules. They, just like Timothy did, often use the puppets, play figures, and dollhouse, not to mention toy guns and emergency vehicles.

Exactly how much imagination do they put into their efforts and play? How would I know? How could I measure that? All I can know for certain is that in the patient and welcoming atmosphere of my office, these children play and create, often in the service of addressing and coping with their lives and demands, as when a young boy with Asperger's attempted to deal with his parents' imminent divorce by building two homes connected by one tunnel through which he shuttled back and forth.

What constitutes creative play, and who is the judge of that? I can tell you that a child who is with an adult who disbelieves in her creativity or who judges it to be lacking will keep her play to herself. That "expert" will feel confirmed in the conviction that, there it is, the child with Asperger's is uncreative. But that expert will be sadly and sorely mistaken.

Creativity does not have to happen fast or loud or colorfully. It's not limited to oil paints or pottery clay. It can be in the form of writing, or punning, or collecting. How about a child who only pretends to be a famed musician, playing an air guitar. Do I have to hear real music to know that they are imagining something creative and joyful (and dreamy)? I agree with Jean-Paul Bovee, a former child with autism and now a historian and library scientist, who wrote: "Imagination is something that is different in a person. For me, it was making my lists, creating genealogies of characters, planning imaginary ball games with baseball cards, creating different languages, and the list goes on" (Donnelly and Bovee 2003, p.476).

Think of it. How many of us make a living being artistic creators? Even of those few who write, paint, and make music, a tiny fraction earn their keep doing so. And yet, look at all of the other kinds of creativity that enrich our lives. It is creative applications of an intellect that advance science, social science, and every other field. Are innovative companies, products, and business plans not acts of creativity? Creativity abounds in every field, whether artistic, or library science, or accounting, or computer science, or you name it. Creativity goes into our recipes and the ways we set up our gardens. Every time any of us have an idea, we are being creative.

There is an endless opportunity in this world for the creative potential and powers of the child with Asperger's. The danger is not in their lacking such creativity and imagination, but in the squelching, the killing off, the neglecting of their creativity. The true danger is that these children come to believe that they are not creative, that they have nothing unique to offer the world and the rest of us. Losing confidence in and enthusiasm for their creative strivings is the real peril.

And it is not just in terms of their future productivity or vocation, though those are important. We want the child with Asperger's to enjoy and feel abuzz with her creativity in everyday life. We want her to flex her humor muscles and be playful in language. We want her to feel comfortable taking risks with playful affection, creative conversing, and as she grows older, flirty teasing. As an adult, we wish her to feel creatively able and eager to decorate her room or home, to arrange flowers, and dress with pizzazz or dignity to suit her tastes.

How can you feed a child's creativity?

- Create space for it to happen. The play and creativity of the child with Asperger's takes time to unfold and blossom. You probably will not see it in a minute's time or under the pressure to produce. That it may go slower does not diminish its value. When we eat a wonderful dinner, do we care how long the chef took to cook it? Whether sudden or prolonged, acts of creativity are equally precious.

- Look for creativity—*everywhere*. Don't be tricked to think it can only be found in the art room or the dollhouse. Allow yourself to see it in the child's growing list of mythical and made-up creatures of the fantastic world he's imagining. See it in the newfangled words she creates to express what things feel like to her. See it in the pipe cleaner web he twists together to keep spiders out of the room. See it in her 4000-plus collection of movie soundtracks, particularly in the clever way she indexes her many MP3s. See it in the jokes he tells, or the way he reorganizes the supply closet.

- Pique your curiosity. Hans Asperger recognized that such children "have the ability to see things and events around them from a new point of view, which often shows superior maturity" (1944/1991, p. 71). Listen for and appreciate the creativity in the child's perspective or worldview or the fresh way that he describes or reacts to some event or experience.

- Invite playfulness and imagination, without demand. Research shows that while they may display less spontaneous pretend play, children with Asperger's, when prompted or given support to do so, show imaginative and symbolic play (Charman and Baron-Cohen 1997; Jarrold 2003; Jarrold, Boucher and Smith 1996; Sherratt 2002). Just the opportunity for a nondirected play experience can raise the frequency of pretend play (Josefi and Ryan 2004). In other words, just providing a safe and open space in which to play or create, again without demand, can bring out playfulness and creativity.

- Make creativity and play a priority. A driven or singular hyperfocus on a behavioral or educational goal, while at times warranted, can obstruct or deter creative impulses and activity. Temporarily, for example, lay aside your goal of teaching etiquette or proper English so that you can give your full attention to what the child is (creatively) telling you. Or perhaps, at least allow yourself to enjoy a joke or tangent or creative diversion and then, once it has run its course and been shared enjoyably by you and the child, matter-of-factly get back on track.

- Watch out for perfectionism. Children with Asperger's are prone to be perfectionists. Don't be led astray by careless or sloppy work. Sometimes that is a red herring that distracts you from the frustration the child feels when performing less than perfectly. Perfectionism, of course, tells the child that making mistakes is a bad thing. But parents and teachers know that mistakes are merely the stepping stones to learning. Worthwhile learning has to involve risks and missteps, and that is the space where creativity and play are born.

- Do not think in terms of savant skills. Autistic children, men, and women are often in the media, showing extraordinary seemingly inhuman feats of memory, mathematical calculation, musical talent and so forth. These so-called *savant skills*, rising like "islands of genius" out of a sea of handicaps (Treffert 1989, 2009), are not the average. Nor are they requisite for a child to be seen as special, creative, or productive. Happé and Frith refer to the need to appreciate the "beautiful otherness of the autistic mind" (2009). It is even easier to think of the mind of the child with Asperger's as being like any other child's, worthy, in all of its glory and lesser things, to be fully enriched, challenged, and admired.

- Appreciate sensory sensitivities. We already discussed the ways in which sensory sensitivities can burden and disrupt children with Asperger's. Such sensory gifts, however, can also trigger and fuel creativity, new and fresh ways of looking at old and familiar experiences. The sensory synesthesia that is common in such children—experiencing, for example, numbers as imagery, or music as colors— can also lend a mind an utterly novel and unique "palette" from which to create.

- Check out the world. High tech, business, science, and engineering are full of people with Asperger's and so are all of our universities and graduate schools, including those in medicine, psychology, and the arts. Libraries, accounting firms, and banks. You name it, and Asperger's is there, producing and creating for all of our benefit. It does imply a range of normalcy, doesn't it?

15

CONSIDERING GIRLS

Do you recall Nellie from early on the book? She was the elementary school-aged girl who sat quietly midst the hustling playground reading and re-reading a series of books about a group of girls (and friends) who lived in the Back Bay neighborhood of Boston. I mentioned her only briefly back then, so let me tell you more about her.

Nellie was a very bright girl who was often extremely moody and irritable. She threw tantrums that shook her home and parents. In spite of her significant intelligence, homework stressed her substantially and led to "meltdowns" that distressed and perplexed her parents. They described Nellie as having to exert utter control over them and everything at home. She, they said, opposed and disrupted most every demand and transition of home life, from getting ready for school until bedtime. Everything was a struggle. But for all of this difficulty, home life was not what motivated Nellie's parents to bring her to therapy.

Nellie had no friends.

School staff observed that Nellie spent her school days virtually alone, not an easy thing to do in a good school system that prided itself on a model of strong community and cooperation. Any free moment—such as recess or lunch—Nellie spent reading. She always carried a book with her, and once in a socially unstructured period, she'd quickly find a spot to plunk down and read, seemingly oblivious to the whirlwind of fun and games that went on around her. Teachers said that even when they did team projects, Nellie barely interacted. During such group projects, she would typically complain to the teacher that she was the only one doing any work or that other children were distracting her by fooling around and laughing.

Just as has been described by Attwood (2006, 2007), Faherty (2006), and others, Nellie did not fit the typical profile for Asperger's, the one I'd gotten accustomed to in my caseload which was predominantly made up of boys. She was not aggressive and did not cause any kind of commotion or behavioral trouble in the classroom. She ever minded her own business, at the slightest hint of free time immersing herself in a book. To onlookers, such as school staff, she appeared to make no effort to engage her peers, though her occasionally remarking "No one likes me" to her mother at bedtime gave a good hint that she was aware of and unhappy with her social plight.

The literature, when compared to more general studies of Asperger's (and boys), is comparatively limited, and yet the facts seem clear. Girls are diagnosed with Asperger's or spectrum disorders much less frequently than are boys (Attwood 2007). Both Attwood (2006) and Faherty (2006) offer what seem to be likely reasons for this discrepancy. Their reasons include: girls tend not to be as behaviorally disruptive as can the boys; girls' impairments can appear subtler; and, given the lesser obvious pressure to get them help, parents might be less willing to pursue a developmentally significant diagnosis for their child. Most intriguing and worrisome, girls, they say, often display behaviors (eye aversion, extreme shyness, and so forth) that are considered "normal" for, well, girls. Carley, in writing about a young Chinese girl, noted too the cultural aspects of diagnosis; in that child's case, "a girl who sat quietly by herself, reading books, and who didn't want anything to do with peers or noisy play [...] was the perfect little girl" (2008, p.48). The bottom line, perhaps, is that girls with Asperger's do not make waves and loud noise in the way that many boys with Asperger's can, the squeaky wheel and that sort of thing.

Attwood (2007) details, too, how the obsessive interests of girls typically differ from boys' preoccupations. Whereas boys might be accumulating miniature cars, endlessly creating mythical hybrids, or studying medieval weaponry, girls with Asperger's often devote themselves to doll play, a love of animals, and reading fiction. Their pretend play can center itself, so writes Faherty, around "princesses, fantasy kingdoms, unicorns, and animals" (2006, p.11), play that on the surface isn't so qualitatively distinct from that of neurotypical girls. Likewise, girls with Asperger's are prone to spend great amounts of free time reading, especially classic literature and books involving animals and fantasy. That their interests are more neurotypical likely means they call less attention to themselves, to the child, and to diagnosis and intervention. But, just because they go unnoticed or undetected—just because they fade into the "invisible end of the spectrum" (Ruth Baker, as quoted in Attwood 2007, p.48)—these girls are spared little of the social isolation, loneliness, despair, and so on that their male counterparts suffer.

As one might anticipate, adolescence can be an especially trying and painful time for girls with Asperger's. Their changing bodies and sexuality can be an extremely stressful and confusing experience, one that well may continue right through adulthood. A lesser concern with fashion and personal hygiene can socially wreak more havoc for girls than for boys, in terms of ostracizing, and shunning. Teens with Asperger's, who have trouble reading social cues, can feel helplessly defenseless in protecting themselves from the bullying, teasing, and sexual aggression of others. Their social impairments and associated fears can also lead these girls to see danger or threat where it doesn't exist, making adolescence a prolonged period of dread and fear.

With a wish to just fit in and be safe from ridicule and loneliness, teenage girls with Asperger's can *masquerade*, presenting themselves, posing, as someone they are not, for example, imitating social behaviors or dialogue that they don't otherwise mean or get (Carrington *et al.* 2003, p.216). With poignancy and the clarity of insight, adult writers with Asperger's have described childhoods and lifetimes of trying to be someone else, making clear their ultimately finding that genuine happiness and self-acceptance comes from being just who they are (Willey 1999). If the much-needed women's movement and psychology of girls' development has taught us anything, we can only imagine the stress and strain of keeping up such appearances, only more so for the child or teen with Asperger's.

Throughout her wonderful book, *Aspergirls*—an essential guide for such girls—Rudy Simone (2010) hammers home the point that, above all, girls with

Asperger's need to honor their authentic and true selves, and so should the parents and teachers who stand beside them. In a particularly rich chapter, aptly titled "Why Smart Girls Sometimes Hate School," Simone urges these girls to hold tight to their passions and interests, to their beings.

But even more than having her interests and talents go undernourished, being teased, bullied, and shunned can savagely tear at and undermine a young girl's being. "I was teased constantly. And I didn't understand why my peers weren't accepting me, why they wouldn't let me be their friend" (Amy Gravino, as quoted by Carley 2008, p.88). "I would be picked on a lot, called names, 'You're ugly,' 'You're stupid' […] I didn't get it. I was like, 'What am I doing wrong?'" (April Malone, as quoted by Carley 2008, p.89).

Simone does not mince words when discussing the responsibility of parents and teachers to protect such children from the bullying and teasing that, we now know, can have an absolutely malignant effect on a child's developing sense of self. "While a good teacher is an incredible gift to a child's life and mind," Simone writes, "a bad one is a force of destruction" (2010, p.29). By "bad," Simone means a teacher who does not protect the child, a teacher who either condones bullying or at least who looks the other way, leaving the child helpless. "You *must*," Simone goes on to address parents, "protect your children" (p.34), suggesting the enormously negative impact that years of bullying and unstimulating instruction can have on a bright and vulnerable girl with Asperger's.

As parents and teachers, though, it is not the epidemiology and incidence rates according to gender that will capture either your attention or interest. What will do that are the individual children before you. Whether male or female, they, like their neurotypical peers, will present a complex profile of being and behaviors that all at once can look familiar and unique. Your aspiration is simply to do your best to see the child clearly and to meet her needs.

What can you do to specifically meet the needs of a girl with Asperger syndrome?

- Assimilate and accommodate. We know that boys and girls with Asperger's can look—and can be—a lot alike and a lot unlike each other. It probably doesn't surprise any of us that the differences are not perfectly black and white. Individual girls with Asperger's, for instance, can be loud and disruptive, just as boys with Asperger's can be gentle, quiet, and hidden behind a persona. Aspire to be open to seeing all sorts of behavior and ways in the child you know. Strive to come up with your own unique and individualized concept and definition for Asperger's to fit the individual child.

- Look deeper. It is not only the public, or parents and teachers who can have trouble seeing the ways that Asperger's manifests itself in a girl. We clinicians encounter the exact same difficulty. We need to look beyond the stereotypes and assess things like: what the child's social connections are; her ways of coping; her interests and passions; her emotional experiences; her ways of communicating; and, not to be neglected, what it feels like being with her. When it comes to diagnosis or understanding a child, we cannot have too much data from all sources.

- Develop evolving criteria. This applies mostly to teachers and other school professionals. Research suggests that girls are under-diagnosed with Asperger's, which is tragic. For this implies that girls are not getting the early help that boys get and which has been shown to be critical, that is, if they get the help at all. And, of course, that these girls are needlessly suffering even one extra day on their own is too much. Help to enlighten others as to the ways that girls with Asperger's can pass under the radar of detection and intervention.

- Think not just Asperger's but girls too. The relatively new insights into the psychological development of girls and women have been a godsend for all of us. Notions of the false self and of ways in which girls and women have sacrificed their authentic beings to fit into society have "saved" girls. (Its lessons, by the way, have also illumined much about life for boys and men.) While the girl you know may well need her Asperger's recognized and dealt with, she at least equally needs her girl development attended to. And, so it seems, the two are intimately related and confounding.

- Monitor and protect against bullying. School can be a tough place for a girl or teen with Asperger's. Such girls and teens need support as they try to navigate waters that can be treacherous, a metaphor that is in no way overstated or unjustified. Keep in mind the minefield that adolescence can be for the average neurotypical teen and multiply it. Stay alert to your daughter's or pupil's social experiences at school. If it includes bullying or mean girl teasing, get active in helping the child to protect herself. Enlist teachers and other school staff to help make the environment safe. Parents and teachers, work together to integrate or build programs that help such children deal with the social demands and dangers of peer culture, and that give the child or teen safety or refuge when she feels lost or that she is in peril.

- Offer the tween or teen girl with Asperger's sources for intellectual understanding of adolescent life. Lisa Iland, as a teenager in high school, "began writing a book about the unspoken rules that compromise the teen social code" (2006, p.33). She describes her motivation as being the sister to a brother with Asperger's and to having friends who are girls with Asperger's. Her chapter titled "Girl to Girl: Advice on Friendship, Bullying, and Fitting In" is an eminently pragmatic, readable, and helpful guide for the girl— and probably boy, too—who has Asperger's (2006, pp.33–63). In her chapter she covers in detail subjects such as: "4 essential areas to know in order to fit in;" "understanding where you fit in—social structures;" "the popularity hierarchy;" "levels of relationships;" "how typical girls show interest;" and much, much else. It is a brilliant guide that perfectly appeals to the girl with Asperger's intellect and interest, serving as a field-guide treatise to how girls behave and interact in the wild. Share it with the girl with Asperger's whom you know (and maybe boy, too), and discuss it, discuss it, discuss it…

16

OTHER CHILDREN'S VIEWS

We have now devoted a good deal of effort and attention to the perspectives of children with Asperger's, their parents, and their teachers. Our work has been worth it, and will, I hope, lead to good things for the children as well as the adults who strive to better understand and be there for them. But yet, we are left with one other viewpoint that cannot help but play a significant role in the experience and, perhaps, immediate or eventual fate of the child with Asperger's. I, as the chapter title has already given away, refer to other children, the peers that the child with Asperger's shares a school and a planet with.

Watching a child with Asperger's navigate the school yard can be a disheartening thing, for both teacher and especially parents. They often observe a child who appears to roam lost and alone, a sight made that much more pained and stark in contrast to the happy and playing children that seem to be everywhere. What do these other children make of the child with Asperger's? Do they even notice?

My listening to parents, teachers, and the children with Asperger's themselves has convinced me what you already know, that there are many possibilities as to how other children can view and treat the child with Asperger's.

In the best of worlds, there are peers, actual children, who somehow get it, who understand and respect the child with Asperger's. They recognize the child's kindness, naivety, and the honesty—without inclination to take advantage of or ridicule it. These peers realize the child has a disorder or challenge that is not his fault. What accounts for such compassion and understanding? Some children have been raised that way, and many, I've learned from my work, have themselves grown up with disabled siblings, an experience that often invokes the best in a loving brother or sister.

But, wondrous as such children can be, we know that this is not playground business as usual. The facts tell us that a vast majority of children with Asperger's experience some degree of teasing or bullying (Little 2002; Shtayermman 2007). This maltreatment over time can erode a child's self-esteem and lead to significant emotional trauma (Juvonen, Graham and Schuster 2003; Kim, Koh and Leventhal 2005). The problem, pervasive and potentially damaging, demands that we try to learn what we can from the perspectives of the peers who, it seems, can be agents for good or bad in the lives of children with Asperger's.

Though almost 20 years old and focused on attitudes toward disabilities in general, the research (as reviewed by Berkson 1993) shows us much that applies to children with Asperger's. As we might guess, peers' attitudes depend, in large measure, on the children with Asperger's themselves, what they are like and how they behave, including how they treat other children. Disabled children who play well, share, are athletic, are affectionate and verbally tactful appear socially appealing in spite of their disability. But this seldom describes children with Asperger's who look different in how they move, play, talk, and interact. In short, the typical traits of Asperger's make children stick out and make them easy targets. While the research suggests that girls tend to be more tolerant, the now well-recognized prevalence and subtleties of mean girl behavior undercuts our confidence in too readily dismissing the reactions of female peers as irrelevant or benign.

This research comes to consensual conclusions that will surprise none of us. The more visible the handicap, the more negative are peers' perceptions and attitudes. Peers perceived children with "strange" behaviors more negatively than children with more comprehensible physical handicaps (Swaim *et al.* 2001). More overtly disruptive behaviors, such as screaming and aggression, leads to more active rejection, whereas more socially withdrawn behavior leads mostly to social neglect. The more "different" a child appears to be, the less likelihood for acceptance and the greater likelihood for social ostracizing. Conversely, the more that the child with disabilities is perceived to be like peers themselves, the better chance for tolerance and liking. Most important of all, the less that peers realize and understand about the nature of a disability, the more they will be prone to misperceive, dislike, and mistreat the child. As I will soon elaborate, this holds promise for the social experience of children with Asperger's.

This research validates our own anecdotal observations and common sense. The child with Asperger's who minds his own business fares better (though that is hardly a free pass from bullying or teasing). The socially awkward child who busts in loudly is bound to suffer some backlash and reverberations, especially in pursuit of less understanding and less kindly peers. Oft times I've found that the child with Asperger's is particularly mistreated by children who have their own issues many of whom are themselves learning disabled or socially challenged. Who better for insecure children to pick on than another child whose behaviors and difficulties seem to be exaggerated examples of their own issues? Bullies, we know, look for the weak and powerless, and unfortunately, many other children follow suit, mostly out of self-protection, a hope that they will not be next on the bully's hit list.

I have learned many times, from the children with Asperger's themselves, that they receive mistreatment after taking a shot at social connection that goes very awry, often one that was originally poorly thought out and misread. Some peers react poorly to the child with Asperger's as a result of the personal discomfort they experience with a child they neither understand nor can manage. For example, in working with teenagers with Asperger's, both boys and girls, I've seen their being teased and rejected, not so much by bad kids, but by apparently neurotypical classmates who were embarrassed and overwhelmed by my patients' obvious and overt interest in them. Likewise, I've seen younger boys and girls mistreat a child with Asperger's because they do not know how to "nicely" get him to listen, not barge in, or not push himself into a social situation. That such children can baffle grown adults should tell us something about the perceptions and reactions of children yet struggling with their own identities and self-images.

The problem clearly lies on both sides of the fence, within the child with Asperger's *and* within peers who may be neurotypical or, frequently, who have their own issues or disabilities. What does that complexity mean for you, the parent or teacher, and what does it suggest you might do to help?

- Be tolerant. To repeat myself, if children with Asperger's can perplex you—a skilled, intelligent, loving, and dedicated adult—how can it not pose a comparable or greater challenge to children yet reckoning to figure themselves out? Children who are themselves troubled, more so those whose own difficulties resonate with those of the child with Asperger's, are especially likely to misperceive and bully. While you will do all you can to counter or forbid such mistreatment, keeping the perpetrator's perspective and vulnerabilities in mind may help you to find solutions.

- Be aware. We agree that social inclusion is mostly a good thing, at least for much of a child's day. Research suggests what daily life seems to tell us, that the child with Asperger's benefits from contact and sharing a world with all kinds of children— whether neurotypical, with other disabilities, or on the spectrum. The greater openness and freedom of today's educational environment means that children with Asperger's may find themselves in less structured and overseen situations where they're more susceptible to social mishap and mistreatment.

- Be a gentle intervener. It is easy to overreact to social mixups or bad reactions on peers' part. However, until shown to be a pattern or with cruel intent, work to use your supervisory powers subtly and discreetly. When seeing some incident brewing, walk calmly through it, separating the children and, perhaps, helping shed some light on the matter. Bringing insight and forgiveness may do more than a prematurely harsh punishment or censure. Of course, this is a matter of prudence; some bullying children will need strong and clear admonishing.

- Foster socially valuable skills in the child with Asperger's. Though, for example, the child's love of videogames may drive you crazy, skill at such a common childhood and adolescent interest can carry some social weight. I have many patients whose connections with other children, as well as their neurotypical siblings' friends, often occur within a context of electronic gaming.

- Model acceptance. This may sound too obvious to state aloud, maybe even offensive. I apologize if so. The more acceptance and dignity you show the child with Asperger's, the more the students will show the same to that child.

- Work with the child. It goes almost without saying that any intervention that can add to the child's social comprehension and skills can help to prevent social problems and hardship. Even as you work to counter bullying and mean girl behaviors, you work to make the child herself less of a target and more of a good companion or school "colleague," or at least one less provocative or out there.

- Lend understanding. Research is clear that the more children understand about the nature of the child's problem, the better. Offering both information and skills (Lewis and Doorlag 2006) can help train young peers to be more accepting and kinder to the child with Asperger's. Both description and explanation can persuasively communicate understanding of Asperger's to neurotypical peers (Campbell 2006; Campbell *et al.* 2004), such that they come to see the child as more like than unlike themselves.

- Be tough, when necessary. As I related in the previous chapter on girls, children with Asperger's can suffer social teasing and rejection that risks destroying their already shaky self-esteems. As responsible parents and teachers, you do all you can to minimize the occurrence of such baleful attitudes and behaviors. But when you cannot prevent them, Simone makes clear that it is your responsibility to protect the child with Asperger's (2010).

- Follow the research. As a parent or teacher, you have more than enough to fill your hands and occupy your days. I know that. But this is an area that holds so much potential—both good and bad—for the child with Asperger's. Google it or use library databases to find out what you can about current research on changing children's attitudes toward disabilities in general and Asperger's or autism in particular. Find out more about promising outcomes or, perhaps, seek ways to bring that information and training to the school where you teach or your child attends.

17

BUTTERFLY LOVE

Okay, it's time for some free association. I say, "butterfly," and you let your mind go. If your childhood was anything like mine, you see yourself in a striped polo shirt stalking black-and-orange Monarchs through field grass up to your waist. Somehow your sneaking up on them is never quiet and slow enough. The butterflies you think of probably come in every size, color, and shape, unsurprising given there are over 25,000 different kinds. And, like the ones I see, not easily caught. Easily frightened, blown away, and harmed.

You get the point. I admit it. I'm hammering you on the head with a creature weighing a hundredth of an ounce. But it's a message that can't be overdone. Children with Asperger's are a lot like butterflies. For some of you, this is hardly news for you know a sweet, gentle, painfully reserved child. Other readers shake their heads at my metaphor. They look across the living room or classroom to that boisterous, awkward, intruding, messy, aggressive, interrupting, crashing, [fill in the blank] child. Bull in a china shop, pint-sized bulldozer, out of control puppy, computer-driven robot? But that is what children show us on the outside, the behavior that can be seen by all.

I am talking about the child's insides, where a majority of children with Asperger's are wary, fragile, and fleeting. We know how hard it is to catch butterflies. It's as if the more we want to hold and know one up close, the more elusive they become. In a paradox that is so much of nature, it is only when we grow tired or bored, when we put down our nets and sit quietly on a country log or city curb, that a butterfly approaches, fluttering by to see who we are and what we are up to. Should we sit still long enough, that butterfly might even stop to rest on our sweater sleeve or pant leg.

If our excitement gets the better of us, and we move fast to grab it, the butterfly will flee and will not return for some time, maybe never. But if can contain ourselves and move slowly enough, our actions showing that we mean it no harm, the butterfly may stay, sometimes for a long while. And that beautiful and delicate butterfly will return to us, again and again, as we prove to be a safe and reliable fixture in the landscape.

As a clinician who's worked with such children for 30 years now, I know firsthand what it's like to connect with them. Getting to know these wonderfully rich and complex boys and girls, young men and women, takes time and patience. I've learned the hard way that trying to rush it along only sets us back and sends away the very child I am trying to reach. Just as well they have taught me that every ounce of care and steadfastness I put into that effort to join them pays off handsomely in the future, nurturing the hour by hours in which we together build relationships that ever grow stronger, more trusting, and more fulfilled.

The view and approach that I have taken great pain to present as it is, as it was shown to me by the children themselves, can best be viewed as a cloud of attitude, a mist of openness, or an aura of possibility that—never to replace the good and powerful methods of education, social pragmatics, speech and language therapy, and so on—hover above and alongside, catalyzing all those worthy interventions can do, all the while nurturing relationships and, more so, the child we meet within them.

Both parents and teachers have noble goals and ambitions that they hold for the child with Asperger's. With love and professional dedication, maybe both, you attend to the child with all of your might in hopes of helping bring him or her to new "places," meaning the acquiring of new and advanced skills, experiences, resiliencies. You realize the peril in seeing a child mostly as a syndrome of autistic behaviors or a bag of undesirable traits to be extinguished, trained, or scripted away. You know well the peril in constantly telling a child that she is not okay as she is, that she should be a different kind of being. Instead you believe deeply that, however much some aspects of Asperger's seem to make a child different, she is qualitatively human, more like than unlike any other child. Even as you try to teach her new skills and ways, you strive to ever honor and respect the child as she is right now, this very moment.

Perhaps, that is it at its most basic. Maybe our greatest role is to not change the child, but to create the conditions, the space, and the relationships in which the child can grow and be, ever more and better in ways that thoroughly resonate with her own wishes and ambitions, her own dreams and yearnings, her own desires and needs.

Back in the 1940s Hans Asperger fell in some kind of love with these children, whether intellectual or emotional or both, he let his curiosity fall for these children over whom he experienced great interest and worry. And yet, for all of his insight and his knowing the hard fates in store for many of the children at his clinic, he knew that their futures and hopes lay as much in our gaining understanding (and appreciation) for them as in changing their behaviors. For all of his clinical acumen and mission, and his sharp and realistic awareness of their limitations, Dr. Asperger surrendered completely to their charms and their possibilities.

Try to let yourself do the same.

- Value honesty and be sincere. If children with Asperger's tend to be anything, it is honest. They abhor white lies, and value less people who are not honest, especially to them. Some say that the Asperger brain is wired for honesty; the child cannot be otherwise but sincere (Baron-Cohen 2007). But that doesn't mean they deserve any less credit for their candor and intellectual integrity. It is theirs, and they should be proud owners of it. Hans Asperger (1944) had already noted that the children in his clinic could instantly see through a teacher's feigning sincerity. Being genuine is an enormous asset when parenting or teaching such a child. They will know if you like or dislike them.

- Seek meaning. I've said it many times already. The conventional wisdom in autism has tended to believe that much of what children with Asperger's say is autistically derived static. The children I've known have taught me otherwise. In his courageous and moving memoir *Running with Walker* (2003), Robert Hughes describes how he and his wife sought meaning in all of their son's behaviors: "Anything that Walker did, no matter how dark or weird, was given a positive—often desperately positive—spin" (p.136). Little is more exciting than deciphering a meaning or message that a child's confusing words or actions intend to convey.

- Use better words. It is commonplace for parents and teachers to react to children's actions and words with a reflexive and nagging: "That's not appropriate." "We don't do that, it's inappropriate." Imagine, if you can, what it would feel like for your spouse or partner, boss, parent, or friend to say that to you, repeatedly? Maybe it is my own thick skin that is talking now, but it seems that saying inappropriate cannot but begin to rub the child the wrong way and, maybe, even give the unintended message that the whole child is inappropriate. There are countless gentler, more accurate, and creative ways to say the same thing to a child.

- Nurture kernels. I have hammered this point home too many times, perhaps. Whatever the trait or skill you seek to improve, find it, hang on to it, and feed it. Whether we are talking about the child's empathy, playfulness, creativity, reading, and so on, work nurturingly with what is there. Proceed with caution, of course, but proceed!

- Remember those baby steps. Parenting or teaching a child with Asperger's can be a slow, quiet enterprise. (I refer to the process not the noise level of the child.) Though growth can come steady, it tends to come slower than inch by inch. It is human for parents and teachers to want to see signs that their efforts are doing something worthwhile, and it's good science to watch for and measure the gains or losses that come. When watching for progress, however, be sure to narrow the scope of your field and use a ruler that fits the scale. Seeing and holding on to the child's progress, however small and snail-paced, is critical. It enables you to keep the child's growth on your radar, and both buoys and guides tomorrow's efforts.

- Be a shepherd. It is easy to get into nose-to-nose battles. Consider backing off. Think of yourself as a shepherd who guides with a firm and soft hand, with wisdom and respect, with confidence and contained positive energy. You don't want a child to jump at your command out of fear. Stretch skills and experiences gently, nudging and prodding with care, patience, and acceptance for the child's reaction to what you are doing. It's a skill. Some parents and teachers have it made in the shade, or so it looks to the rest of us. Parenting or educating children seems to come easy, as if they were born to the job. Their every interaction seems natural and right on, as if they have some kind of inborn sixth sense or intuition for the task and the child. Most of us, unfortunately, are not so well endowed. Most parents and teachers have to acquire these same skills. The good news, however, is that skills can be improved as long as one wants to work at them. Practice them, for skills, like muscles, need regular exercise.

- Be an experimenter. Take risks. You need not wait for developmental psychologists or educational researchers to show you how to intervene. If you have a hunch as to a way to better reach the child, teach him reading, get her engaged in physical activity, get him to listen try it and so forth—*try it out*. Trial and error is a tried and true method for progress. Instead of beating yourself up for mistakes, or retreating from them, see them as necessary and promising opportunities to learn and move ahead. You have everything you need—you and the child— to do such research.

- Appreciate your powers and influence. This book is not a joke, and so it has no punchline. But if it did have one, it would be the simple message that you, parent and teacher, wield great power and relevance in the life of a child with Asperger's. You hold the most profound influence over the child who looks to you for safety, caring, direction, and responsiveness. Whatever the context or task at hand, you are ever an instrument of relating that can be played, by yourself, to endless heights and possibilities.

18

CONNECTING
IT ALL

It's been 65 years since Hans Asperger introduced the world formally to a group of children who were all at once intelligent, learning disabled, articulate, unexpressive, socially awkward, and so forth. Even then, Dr. Asperger recognized that these children were special and distinct, that they deserved thorough and sophisticated testing that realized and accommodated how that testing would itself would be difficult, that they deserved apt education by teachers who were skilled, emotionally attuned, sincere, and interested in the children; and that they were, above all, like other children in that they had to deal with the psychological tasks of growing up, the tragedies and misfortunes of life, on and on, that all children must confront. Understanding, *even then*, that Asperger's is a disorder based in biology, specifically neurology and the brain, Dr. Asperger held compassion for parents who he knew needed support not blame. Most of all, Dr. Asperger knew that Asperger's, especially with its social impairment and disadvantages, could lead to a lifetime of isolation, hardship, and despair. Though an explosion of research and knowledge about Asperger's is buoying all of us, the reality remains. Asperger's "profoundly limits a child's participation in this process of growing up" (Szatmari 1991, p.74).

Children with Asperger's enter the world with fewer resources to communicate, socially relate, and deal with feelings. As if these burdens are not enough, they, in turn, lead to secondary deficits, in the way that carrying on with a bum knee can later cause hip and back problems. Being different, these children are then rejected, depriving them of the social experiences and practice that would ironically help them learn to do it (socially) better. At the end of the day, all of these factors add up to an existence in which children with Asperger's are certain to go to bed each night having not gotten much, if any, of the validation, admiration, empathy, and understanding that their neurotypical peers routinely enjoy. It is with this background and backdrop that children with Asperger's meet you, their parents and teachers.

To best fulfill that precious and noble privilege and duty is what this book has been about. And so, you, parent and teacher, will continue to do your best to nudge and stretch the child along, ever aspiring to the next step while honoring the step, and way, that the child is right this very moment. Your exquisite realization for the importance of sheer human dignity, especially for such a vulnerable group of children, will ever guide your efforts to reform or educate the child. You will seek the child's innate gifts and nurture them with all your might. Whether they are contemplating species of goldfish or a possible career choice, you will care what it is that they think and want or wonder about, ever trying to "understand [their] perspective, communicate it, [and] work together to bring awareness, solution, or acceptance" (Jacobsen 2003).

Knowing what the child with Asperger's faces, you will take seriously their feelings, their anxieties and depressions, listening and affirming their predicaments, helping them take and engage in steps to relieve or assuage such hurts. One unnecessary day of their suffering, we agree, is too much, much too much. But, attending to ways that their Asperger's causes them hurdles and distress won't distract you from other things, such as their coping with ordinary developmental tasks, chronic illness and tragedies, abuse and neglect. Being attuned to their Asperger experience will not divert you from noticing when, for instance, they confront a new and different dilemma or pressure, ordeals that, big or small, may have nothing at all to do with their neurological disorder.

You will realize that their opinions matter, not as autistic rambling, but as their precious thoughts for they are theirs and all they have. Above all, you will foster relationships, the safety and nourishment of which implicitly encourage them to unfold and blossom, to take risks, and to show who they are with less fear and greater openness. You will do all you can to hold them in ways that invite their becoming all they can be, in ways that they value as much or more than you do.

None of us know what the future will bring. Perhaps one day we will unravel the biological mysteries of autism and Asperger's. Perhaps our knowledge will lead to cure and prevention, who can say? Scientific miracles happen. Yet, for all of the hopes and who knows of science and medicine, there is one truth that we can be certain of even now. Whatever technologies and discoveries come ahead for the child with Asperger's, none will ever threaten the basic truth and power that a good and meaningful relationship will hold for such children, most of all children who ever try their best and use their energies to cope in a world that can be too hard, too demanding, and that moves too fast.

I've yet to meet one child with Asperger's who does not equate empathy with understanding, and, in turn, understanding with love. I've countless times seen the eyes of a child with Asperger's well up because I simply got what they meant, *because I simply understood.* What more need I say? What more need we know?

References

American Psychiatric Association (APA) (2000) *Diagnostic and Statistical Manual of Mental Disorders*, 4th Edition (Text Revision). Washington, DC: American Psychiatric Association.

Asperger, H. (1991) "Autism and Asperger Syndrome." In U. Frith (ed. and trans.) *Autism and Asperger Syndrome* (pp.36–92). Cambridge, UK: Cambridge University Press. (Original work published 1944.)

Attwood, T. (2004a) *Exploring Feelings: Cognitive Behavior Therapy to Manage Anger.* Arlington, TX: Future Horizons.

Attwood, T. (2004b) *Exploring Feelings: Cognitive Behavior Therapy to Manage Anxiety.* Arlington, TX: Future Horizons.

Attwood, T. (2006) "The Pattern of Abilities and Development of Girls with Asperger"s Syndrome." In T. Attwood *et al.* (eds) *Asperger's and Girls* (pp.1–7). Arlington, TX: Future Horizons.

Attwood, T. (2007) *The Complete Guide to Asperger's Syndrome.* London: Jessica Kingsley Publishers.

Barnhill, G. (2001) "Social attributions and depression in adolescents with Asperger Syndrome." *Focus on Autism and Other Developmental Disabilities 16*, 1, 46–53.

Baron-Cohen, S. (1987) "Autism and symbolic play." *British Journal of Developmental Psychology 5*, 139–148.

Baron-Cohen, S. (1989) "The autistic child's theory of mind: A case of specific developmental delay." *Journal of Child Psychology and Psychiatry 30*, 2, 285–297.

Baron-Cohen, S. (2003) *The Essential Difference.* New York: Basic Books.

Baron-Cohen, S. (2007) "I cannot tell a lie." *In Character 3*, 52–59.

Baron-Cohen, S. (2008) *Autism and Asperger Syndrome.* Oxford: Oxford University Press.

Bauminger, N. (2004) "The expression and understanding of jealousy in children with autism." *Development and Psychopathology 16*, 157–177.

Bauminger, N., Shulman, C. and Agam, G. (2003) "Peer interaction and loneliness in high-functioning children with autism." *Journal of Autism and Developmental Disorders 33*, 5, 489–507.

Bauminger, N., Chomsky-Smolkin, L., Orbach-Caspi, E., Zachor, D. and Levy-Shiff, R. (2008) "Jealousy and emotional responsiveness in young children with ASD." *Cognition and Emotion 22*, 4, 595–619.

Bauminger, N., Solomon, M., Aviezer, A., Heung, K., Brown, J. and Rogers, S. (2008) "Friendship in high-functioning children with Autism Spectrum Disorder: Mixed and non-mixed dyads." *Journal of Autism and Developmental Disorders 38*, 7, 1211–1229.

Bemporad, J., Ratey, J. and O'Driscoll, G. (1987) "Autism and emotion: An ethological theory." *American Journal of Orthopsychiatry 57*, 477–483.

Ben Shalom, D., Mostofsky, S., Hazlett, R., Goldberg, M., Landa, R., Faran, Y. *et al.* (2006) "Normal physiological emotions but differences in expression of conscious feelings in children with High-Functioning Autism." *Journal of Autism and Developmental Disorders 36*, 3, 395–400.

Berkson, G. (1993) *Children with Handicaps: A Review of Behavioral Research.* Hillsdale, NJ: Erlbaum.

Bogdashina, O. (2003) *Sensory Perceptual Issues in Autism and Asperger Syndrome: Different Sensory Experiences, Different Perceptual Worlds.* London: Jessica Kingsley Publishers.

Bromfield, R. (1989) "Psychodynamic play therapy with a high-functioning autistic child." *Psychoanalytic Psychology 4*, 439–453.

Bromfield, R. (2000) "It's the tortoise race: long-term psychodynamic psychotherapy with a high-functioning autistic adolescent." *Psychoanalytic Inquiry 20*, 732–745.

Bromfield, R. (2010a) *Doing Therapy with Children and Adolescents with Asperger Syndrome.* Hoboken, NJ: Wiley.

Bromfield, R. (2010b) *Playing for Real; Exploring the World of Child Therapy and the Inner Worlds of Children.* Boston: Basil. (Original work published NY: Penguin USA 2001.)

Campbell, J. (2006) "Changing children's attitudes toward autism: A process of persuasive communication." *Journal of Developmental and Physical Disease 18*, 251–272.

Campbell, J.M., Ferguson, J.E., Herzinger, C.V., Jackson, J.N. and Marino, C.A. (2004) "Combined descriptive and explanatory information improves peers' perceptions of autism." *Research in Developmental Disabilities 25*, 321–339.

Carley, M.J. (2008) *Asperger's from the Inside Out.* New York: Perigree.

Carrington, S., Templeton, E. and Papincazak, T. (2003) "Adolescents with Asperger Syndrome and perceptions of friendship." *Focus on Autism and Other Developmental Disabilities 18*, 4, 211–218.

Charman, T. and Baron-Cohen, S. (1997) "Brief report: Prompted pretend play in Autism." *Journal of Autism and Developmental Disorders 27*, 3, 325–332.

Critchley, H., Daly, E., Bullmore, E., Williams, S., Van Amelsvoort, T., Robertson, D. *et al.* (2000) "The functional neuroanatomy of social behaviour: Changes in cerebral blood flow when people with autistic disorder process facial expressions." *Brain: A Journal of Neurology 123*, 11, 2203–2212.

Dawson, G., Osterling, J., Melzoff, A. and Kuhl, P. (2000) "Case study of the development of an infant with autism from birth to 2 years of age." *Journal of Applied Developmental Psychology 21*, 299–313.

de Bruin, E., Ferdinand, R., Meesters, S., de Nijs, P. and Verheij, F. (2007) "High rates of psychiatric co-morbidity in PDD-NOS." *Journal for Autism and Developmental Disorders 37*, 877–886.

Donnelly, J. and Bovee, J. (2003) "Reflections on play: Recollections from a mother and her son with Asperger Syndrome." *Autism 7*, 4, 471–476.

Dubin, N. and Carley, M. (2007) *Asperger's and Bullying: Strategies and Solutions*. London: Jessica Kingsley Publishers.

Faherty, C. (2000) *Asperger's: What Does It Mean to Me?* Arlington, TX: Future Horizons.

Faherty, C. (2006) "Asperger's Syndrome in Women: A Different Set of Challenges?" In T. Attwood *et al.* (eds) *Asperger's and Girls* (pp.9–14). Arlington, TX: Future Horizons.

Fitzgerald, M. and Molyneux. S. (2004) "Overlap between alexithymia and Asperger's Syndrome." *American Journal of Psychiatry 161*, 2134–2135.

Frith, U. (2001) "Mind blindness and the brain in autism." *Neuron 32*, 969–979.

Frith, U., Happé, F. and Siddons, F. (1994) "Autism and theory of mind in everyday life." *Social Development 3*, 108–124.

Ghaziuddin, M., Weidmer-Mikhail, E. and Ghaziuddin, N. (1998) "Comorbidity of Asperger Syndrome: A preliminary report." *Journal of Intellectual Disability Records 42*, 279–283.

Gillberg, C (1991) "Clinical and neurobiological aspects of Asperger Syndrome in six family studies." In U. Frith (ed. and trans.) *Autism and Asperger Syndrome* (pp.122–146). Cambridge, UK: Cambridge University Press.

Gillis, J., Natof, T., Lockshin, S. and Romanczyk, R. (2009) "Fear of routine physician exams in children with autism spectrum disorders." *Focus on Autism and Other Developmental Disabilities 24*, 3, 156–168.

Ginott, H. (2003) *Between Parent and Child.* New York: Three Rivers Press. (Original work published in 1955.)

Grandin, T. (2008) *The Way I See It.* Arlington, TX: Future Horizons.

Hall, K. (2001) *Asperger Syndrome, the Universe and Everything.* London: Jessica Kingsley Publishers.

Happé, F. and Frith, U. (1996) "The neuropsychology of autism." *Brain 119*, 1377–1400.

Happé, F. and Frith, U. (2009) "The beautiful otherness of the autistic mind." *Philosophical Transactions of the Royal Society 364*, 1345–1350.

Harris, P. and Leevers, H. (2000) "Pretending, Imagery and Self-awareness in Autism." In S. Baron-Cohen, H. Tager-Flusberg and D. Cohen (eds) *Understanding Other Minds: Perspectives from Autism and Developmental Cognitive Neuroscience* (pp.182–202). Oxford: Oxford University Press.

Hobson, R., Lee, A. and Hobson, J. (2009) "Qualities of symbolic play among children with autism: A social-developmental perspective." *Journal of Autism and Developmental Disorders 39*, 1, 12–22.

Howe, S. (1996) "Getting smart about gifted kids." *Boston College Chronicle 5*, September 5. Available at www.bc.edu/bc_org/rvp/pubaf/chronicle/v5/S5/winner.html, accessed on September 11, 2009.

Hughes, R. (2003) *Running With Walker*. London: Jessica Kingsley Publishers.

Iland, L. (2006) "Girl to Girl: Advice on Friendship, Bullying, and Fitting In." In T. Attwood *et al.* (eds) *Asperger's and Girls* (pp.33–63). Arlington, TX: Future Horizons.

Jacobsen, P. (2003) *Asperger Syndrome and Psychotherapy*. Philadelphia, PA: Jessica Kingsley Publishers.

Jarrold, C. (2003) "A review of research into pretend play in autism." *Autism 7*, 4, 379–390.

Jarrold, C., Boucher, J. and Smith, P. (1993) "Symbolic play in autism: A review." *Journal of Autism and Developmental Disorders 23*, 2, 281–307.

Jarrold, C., Boucher, J. and Smith, P. (1996) "Generativity deficits in pretend play in autism." *British Journal of Developmental Psychology 14*, 275–300.

Josefi, O. and Ryan, V. (2004) "Non-directive play therapy for young children with autism: A case study." *Clinical Child Psychology and Psychiatry 9*, 4, 533–551.

Juvonen, J., Graham, S. and Schuster, M. (2003) "Bullying among young adolescents: The strong, the weak, and the troubled." *Pediatrics 112*, 1231–1237.

Kanner, L. (1943) "Autistic disturbances of affective contact." *Nervous Child 2*, 217–250.

Kim, Y., Koh, Y. and Leventhal, B. (2005) "School bullying and suicidal risk in Korean middle school students." *Pediatrics 115*, 357–363.

Lampert, K. (2005) *Traditions of Compassion: From Religious Duty to Social Activism.* New York: Palgrave-Macmillan.

Levine, K. and Chedd, N. (2007) *Replays.* Philadelphia, PA: Jessica Kingsley Publishers.

Lewis, R. and Doorlag, D.H. (2006) *Teaching Special Students in General Education Classrooms.* Upper Saddle River, NJ: Pearson Education.

Leyfer, O., Folstein, S., Bacalman, S., Davis, N., Dinh, E., Morgan, J. *et al.* (2006) "Comorbid psychiatric disorders with children with autism: Interview development rates of disorders." *Journal of Autism and Developmental Disorders 36*, 849–861.

Little, L. (2002) "Middle-class mothers' perceptions of peer and sibling victimization among children with Asperger Syndrome and non-verbal learning disorders." *Issues in Comprehensive Pediatric Nursing 25*, 43–57.

Lord, C., Risi, S., Lambrecht, L., Cook, E. Jr., Leventhal, B., DiLavore, P. *et al.* (2000) "The Autism Diagnostic Observation Schedule— Generic: A standard measure of social and communication deficits associated with the spectrum of autism." *Journal of Autism and Developmental Disorders 30*, 3, 205–223.

Markram, H., Rinaldi, T. and Markram, K. (2007) "The intense world syndrome—an alternative hypothesis for autism." *Frontiers in Neuroscience 1*, 77–96.

Mathur, R. and Berndt, T. (2006) "Relations of friends' activities to friendship quality." *Journal of Early Adolescence 26*, 3, 365–388.

Merriam-Webster (1998) *Merriam-Webster's Collegiate Dictionary,* 10th Edition. Springfield, MA: Merriam-Webster.

Minio-Paluello, I., Baron-Cohen, S., Avenanti, A., Walsh, V. and Aglioti, S. (2009) "Absence of embodied empathy during pain observation in Asperger Syndrome." *Biological Psychiatry 65*, 1, 55–62.

Rogers, K., Dziobek, I., Hassenstab, J., Wolf, O. and Convit, A. (2007) "Who cares? Revisiting empathy in Asperger Syndrome." *Journal of Autism and Developmental Disorders 37*, 709–715.

Sainsbury, C. (2000) *Martian in the Playground: Understanding the Schoolchild with Asperger's Syndrome.* Bristol, UK: Lucky Duck Publishing.

Saulnier, C. and Klin, A. (2007) "Brief report: Social and communication abilities and disabilities in higher functioning individuals with autism and Asperger's Syndrome." *Journal of Autism and Developmental Disabilities 37,* 4, 788–793.

Sherratt, D. (2002) "Developing pretend play in children with autism: A case study." *Autism 6,* 2, 169–179.

Shtayermman, O. (2007) "Peer victimization in adolescents and young adults diagnosed with Asperger's Syndrome: A link to depressive symptomatology, anxiety symptomatology and suicidal ideation." *Issues in Comprehensive Pediatric Nursing 30,* 87–107.

Simone, R. (2010) *Aspergirls.* London: Jessica Kingsley Publishers.

Simpson, R. and Myles, B. (1998) "Aggression among children and youth who have Asperger's Syndrome: A different population requiring different strategies." *Preventing School Failure 42,* 4, 149–153.

Sullivan, H. (1953) *The Interpersonal Theory of Psychiatry.* New York: Norton.

Swaim, K.F., Morgan, S.B., Lenhart, J.A., Hyder, K., Zimmerman, A.W. and Pevsner, J. (2001) "Children's attitudes and behavioral intentions toward a peer with autistic behaviors: Does a brief educational intervention have an effect?" *Journal of Autism and Developmental Disorders 31,* 195–205.

Szatmari, P. (1991) "Asperger's Syndrome: Diagnosis, treatment, and outcome." *Psychiatric Clinics of North America 14,* 1, 81–92.

Tantam, D. (1991) "Asperger Syndrome in Adulthood." In U. Frith (ed.) *Autism and Asperger Syndrome* (pp.147–183). New York: Cambridge University Press.

Thede, L. and Coolidge, F. (2007) "Psychological and neurobehavioral comparisons of children with Asperger's disorder versus High-Functioning Autism." *Journal of Autism and Developmental Disorders 37,* 5, 847–854.

Treffert, D. (1989) *Extraordinary People: Understanding Savant Syndrome.* New York: Ballentine.

Treffert, D. (2009) "The savant syndrome: An extraordinary condition—A synopsis: Past, present, future." *Philosophical Transactions of the Royal Society 364*, 1351–1357.

Ungerer, J. and Sigman, M. (1981) "Symbolic play and language comprehension in autistic children." *Journal of the American Academy of Child Psychiatry 20*, 318–337.

Volkmar, F. and Klin, A. (2000) "Diagnostic Issues in Asperger Syndrome." In A. Klin, F. Volkmar and S. Sparrow (eds) *Asperger Syndrome* (pp.25–71). New York: Guilford Press.

Willemsen-Swinkels, S., Bakermans-Kranenburg, M., van Ijzedorn, M., Buitelaar, J. and van Engeland, H. (2000) "Insecure and disorganised attachment in children with a pervasive developmental disorder: Relationship with social interaction and heart rate." *Journal of Child Psychology and Psychiatry 41*, 759–767.

Willey, L. (1999) *Pretending to Be Normal*. London: Jessica Kingsley Publishers.

Wing, L. (1981) "Asperger's syndrome: A clinical account." *Psychological Medicine 11*, 1, 115–129.

Winner, E. (1996) *Gifted Children: Myths and Realities*. New York: Basic.

Witwer, A. and Lecavelier, L. (2008) "Examining the validity of autism spectrum disorder subtypes." *Journal of Autism and Developmental Disorders 38*, 1611–1624.

Wulff, S. (1985) "The symbolic and object play of children with autism: A review." *Journal of Autism and Developmental Disorders 15*, 139–148.

About the Author

Richard Bromfield, Ph.D., is a graduate of Bowdoin College and the University of North Carolina at Chapel Hill. A faculty member of Harvard Medical School, he writes about children, psychotherapy, and family life in both professional and popular periodicals. He is in private practice in Boston, Massachusetts.

He is also the author of *Doing Therapy with Children and Adolescents with Asperger's Syndrome* (Wiley); *Teens in Therapy: Making It Their Own* (W. W. Norton); *Doing Child and Adolescent Psychotherapy* (Wiley); *Playing for Real: Exploring Child Therapy and the Inner Worlds of Children* (Basil); *How to Unspoil Your Child Fast: A Speedy, Complete Guide to Contented Children and Happy Parents* (Sourcebooks); and *How to Write and Cite APA-Style-6th* (Basil).

Subject Index

Author Index